M000236890

PRAISE FOR *FAST FORWARD*

"*Fast Forward* is more than a business book. It's a book on friendship, human connection, and personal growth—in other words, what we need in today's society."

— Scott Galloway, Professor of Marketing, NYU Stern
School of Business, and author of *Adrift*

"I am thrilled that you are about to get the most useful and practical step-by-step guide to having an extraordinary life. I personally use the techniques in this book and they have been life changing. As a leader, I have also seen the difference these principles make in workplace culture and in the lives of thousands of people from my time at Facebook. This book will help you, challenge you, and guide you. It is a true gift."

— Carolyn Everson, Senior Advisor, Permira; Board Director of
The Walt Disney Company, The Coca-Cola Company, and Under
Armour; and former Head of Meta's Global Business Group

"I have personally benefited greatly from *Fast Forward*'s approach and shared it with many colleagues and friends. Their approach is not only inspiring, it's a practical, actionable road map for how to be a better leader and a better human."

— Kristin Lemkau, CEO of US Wealth Management, JPMorgan Chase

"Fast Forward coaching is a key to the success of our top performers. Lisa and Wendy bring their transformative approach to life on the pages of *Fast Forward*. You will walk away with so many insights for your own life!"

— Blake Chandlee, President of Global Business
Solutions, Bytedance/TikTok

"Wow! The magic for the reader is the possibility of getting new perspectives and distinctions that will shift the trajectory of your life, combined with the creation of a plan that will get you moving towards your bold and beautiful goal. Wendy and Lisa's approach, hard earned and honed through working with thousands of clients, can help you radically improve the quality of your life!"

— Scott Blanchard, President, The Ken Blanchard Companies

"Insightful, unique, and actionable. *Fast Forward* offers a proven approach that executives have been learning from Wendy and Lisa for years. Their real-world experience, passion for supporting people's whole lives, and ability to accelerate teams towards audacious goals shines through in their work and in their impact."

—Tara Walpert Levy, VP of Americas, YouTube

"This is a must-read for professionals at all levels. I brought *Fast Forward*'s Power Principles to my team and my podcast. Now you can put their approach into action for your career and life."

— Rebecca Jarvis, financial journalist, ABC News

"*Fast Forward* is packed with inspiration and practical guidance to help you grow your confidence, find your voice and live your best life. Wendy and Lisa did that for me, which inspired me to write my own book. I am thrilled their game-changing approach is now available to anyone!"

—Mita Mallick, Head of Inclusion, Equity, and Impact, Carta; contributing writer, *Harvard Business Review*

FAST
FORWARD

FAST

FORWARD

5 Power Principles to
Create the Life You Want
in Just One Year

WENDY LESHGOLD
and LISA McCARTHY

Matt Holt Books
An Imprint of BenBella Books, Inc.
Dallas, TX

Matt Holt is an imprint of BenBella Books, Inc.
10440 N. Central Expressway
Suite 800
Dallas, TX 75231
benbellabooks.com
Send feedback to feedback@benbellabooks.com

BenBella and *Matt Holt* are federally registered trademarks.

Printed in the United States of America
10 9 8 7 6 5 4 3 2 1

Library of Congress Control Number: 2023003627
ISBN 9781637744000 (hardcover)
ISBN 9781637744017 (electronic)

Copyediting by Leah Baxter
Proofreading by Denise Pangia and Cape Cod Compositors, Inc.
Indexing by WordCo Indexing Services, Inc.
Text design and composition by Aaron Edmiston
Cover design by Brigid Pearson
Cover image © Shutterstock / Ceplus Studio
Printed by Lake Book Manufacturing

Contents

Power Principle 1
DECLARE A BOLD VISION
Throw Your Hat over the Wall

Power Principle 2
CHOOSE A NEW PERSPECTIVE
What's the Cost of Being Right?

Chapter 1

MAKE THIS *YOUR* YEAR

When we met Avery for the first time, the word that came to mind was "frazzled." We would expect somebody in a leadership position at a large company like hers to seem busy or even overwhelmed, but she looked exhausted. Her company had hired us to work with their leaders, through our programs and coaching, and Wendy chose to be Avery's coach. Avery's colleagues had organized meetings with their coaches right away, but it took almost two months for Avery to get started with us.

As they talked, Wendy began to understand why. She asked her usual first questions: Where are you proud and satisfied? Where are you not? What's getting in the way of your happiness, peace, and success?

Out poured the realities of Avery's daily life. She had a ten-month-old daughter, Lily. She lived in the suburbs of Los Angeles, and her job required her to commute almost an hour each way in infuriating traffic. Traveling around the city with the baby, taking turns with her husband to get her to daycare and doctor visits, was a grind. Making things even harder, Avery had to travel at least twice a month for work, which left her feeling exhausted and guilty about not being home.

Avery and her husband had met doing a play together when they were seniors in college, and their love of theater was a big part of their life together. Before becoming parents, they saw a play almost every week with their friends. Since Lily was born, they'd only been to *one* play—on a rare weekend when Avery's parents were in town.

At work, the situation wasn't much better. Avery felt discouraged by the state of her team, by how hard it was to make things happen with her peers, and by the lack of time she had to accomplish important goals. Being a good leader and having a positive impact on people mattered to Avery—deeply—which is why she responded the way she did when Wendy shared some opportunities for growth based on interviews with Avery's team: She lost it. "I'm so frustrated! I'm working so hard, I'm trying so hard, and I still feel like I'm failing as a leader, a mother, a wife."

Avery was so deep in the fog of busyness, she couldn't see beyond the ground right in front of her, the next thing she had to do, the next work crisis she had to manage, the next demand on her time and energy. She felt stuck, resigned to how things were, and not hopeful about achieving her most important ambitions. She couldn't see a path to creating the life she wanted.

Your situation may be nothing like Avery's, but you might *feel* the same. Too many of us do.

Every year, we at Fast Forward Group work with thousands of people who believe that they have to put important goals and people "on hold" until some mythical point in the future when they have more time or their circumstances align just so. They believe that their days and their lives are not within their control—because they spend them reacting to people and situations *outside of* their control. They think, "If I keep making sacrifices and keep pushing forward, eventually I'll arrive in a better place where life is easier and more fulfilling." Not likely.

Next year is not going to be any better—*unless you choose to make it better*. In this book, we're going to show you how.

The five Power Principles we'll share here represent a simple, actionable, *fast* approach to creating the life you want in just one year. They do this by **fundamentally shifting how you relate to your power in the present and what you see as possible in the future.** They have been refined through over a decade of work with people and companies around the globe. Backed by neuroscience, they help bridge the gap between *knowing* and *doing*—between *knowing* things could be better (or *wanting* things to be better) and *doing* the things that create success and happiness in your life.

We can't tell you precisely how to be happy. We don't know what you want or what obstacles you'll have to overcome to get there. But **we can give you a system for fueling your own happiness** that has worked for more than a hundred thousand people and that has been used by leading companies to support their employees' success. Following this system can put you in the driver's seat of your own life, allowing you to feel purposeful and intentional in your choices, rather than reactive or out of control. It's how you can make this year, and every year, your year.

Which is exactly what Avery discovered.

That's what the Power Principles offer: a smoother,
***faster* path to a more fulfilling future of *your* choosing.**

SHIFTING YOUR RELATIONSHIP WITH POWER

Power doesn't always have positive connotations in our world. Phrases like "abuse of power," "power corrupts," and "power trip" send the message that using our power is a straight path to becoming dictators. At the same time, most of us want to feel more empowered. Indeed, recent research suggests that our desire for power is not about control of other people; it's about control of ourselves and our lives, our biological, human desire for autonomy.[1]

Our need for autonomy influences how we feel about our lives. For instance, a survey by the Cato Institute found that 68 percent of people who "*strongly* believe they have personal agency," or feel in charge of the direction their life takes, also feel their lives have meaning and purpose.[2]

Award-winning science journalist David Robson recently wrote, "Whatever their background, people who perceive that they have power to determine their own fate—from tiny short-term decisions to important life events—tend to be happier, healthier and more productive."[3] They also experience less stress when they feel they have some control of the outcome of a situation. Take that feeling *away* and replace it with a sense of helplessness or an inability to change their circumstances and even "small stresses may become exaggerated."

Isn't that how Avery was feeling? Helpless to change her circumstances?

And yet, she really wasn't. It brings to mind a quote from the influential novelist and human rights activist Alice Walker: **"The most common way people give up their power is by thinking they don't have any."** When we make that mistake, our focus shifts to all the things in life we can't control. Our frustration and pessimism climb, and our ability to make progress toward the things we want takes a hit.

When Wendy met with Avery, she noticed that when Avery complained about the circumstances of her life—the travel, the workload, her commute, her too-small apartment—she truly believed these things were outside her control. She was convinced that this was "just the way it is." Avery had recently participated in our Fast Forward program, so she had an idea of what she wanted in her career and personal life, what motivated and inspired her, and what was important. But to create the life she wanted, she still needed to acknowledge the power she had to make them a reality, regardless of her circumstances.

To help, Wendy kept asking her one simple question: **What could you do about it?** At first, Avery's focus was on small, incremental actions. "I could talk to my boss about reducing my travel a bit." "I could find a trusted babysitter." "I could block Saturdays for family time." These simple starting steps created small differences that began to accumulate. More fundamentally, they shifted what Avery believed about her power to shape a different future.

One day, she showed up and said, "There's a job opening in Chicago." As she told Wendy about it, she moved back and forth between all the reasons it would help her achieve what she knew she wanted and all the reasons she might fail or it might not work out. It meant reporting to somebody she didn't know. Would this person support her? Would their visions of how to lead align? She was also making real headway with her team, and she would have to start over, building new relationships. And man, those Chicago winters!

On the other side, she knew the team needed a leader like her, somebody who would advocate for them. The role presented a lot of opportunities for growth. And she wouldn't have to travel much. Living in Chicago also meant being closer to family (more babysitters!), living in a city known for incredible theater, and a much easier commute.

"You know, I wouldn't even be considering this if I hadn't already taken the steps I have—if I didn't have the clarity and feeling of control that I do now," she told Wendy.

Avery decided to take the job, and she absolutely crushed it. The move was a great choice for her family and her marriage. Year by year, she has continued to shape her life to be what she wants it to be. We heard that she had a new baby recently, and we wondered if having an infant to care for again would send her back into the fog of busyness and overwhelm—but it didn't. She now knows how to be intentional with her time and focus. She knows how to chart a course for the year that serves as a north star. She knows how to overcome mental hurdles to making what she wants a priority. She feels confident in her choices. Has her life been all sunshine and rainbows? Of course not. For all of us, the train sometimes goes off the tracks, but Avery has the clarity and tools to get it back on track.

None of Avery's successes would have happened if she hadn't developed the belief that she could *make* them happen—that **even if there was no obvious path to that future life, she had the power to create it.** Any of us can build that same sense of agency and ownership in our lives.

GET CLEAR, BE BOLD, TAKE ACTION

Lisa: In 2012, I walked out of my weekly leadership meeting exasperated. Reorg number twelve had been announced, and this one was the last straw. My manager, who I admired and respected, was being replaced. It was time to go. I handed in my notice . . . and found myself at a crossroads.

The safe path would have been to find another sales leadership role in the same industry. I was good at it, and it would be a comfortable move. My success on that path was predictable, but nothing about it got me excited. It didn't help me focus on my biggest passion and what I've been told is my superpower: inspiring people to believe in themselves and see new possibilities for their future.

For years I had said, "For my chapter two, I'm going to launch a company that helps people be successful and fulfilled professionally and personally." I had watched people play it safe at work, live in a state of overwhelm and stress, and put their personal lives on hold for professional success—waiting to take care of their health and well-being, spend time with people they cared about, or make time for things they loved or that were important. In all my years as a people developer, I hadn't found a program that helped people overcome that challenge. I had experienced it myself, and I knew there was a way through.

While my vision inspired me, I saw it as work I would do "someday"—when I was older, when we weren't saving for both college and retirement, when I didn't have three kids under twelve. When I considered taking the leap sooner rather than later, I felt so much fear. I had always worked in large companies. I didn't know how to start a business. Our financial life and my professional reputation felt at risk. It felt like jumping off a cliff. I was waking up at 5 AM feeling nauseated.

I did what I usually do when I feel stuck. I called my best friend, Wendy, who I'd met at sleepaway camp when we were ten, to talk it through. Wendy was an in-demand executive coach who had spent years as a senior leader in global companies. Like me, she understood firsthand the challenges people face in making their careers and their personal lives everything they want them to be, especially people in high-pressure roles or in fast-paced environments. As we talked, she shared that she was at a crossroads, too. When she had launched her coaching business, she had carefully crafted her life so that she could do everything she wanted. After doing the same work for eleven years, she felt she had more to offer. She wanted to have more impact, to play bigger, and to realize her full career potential.

By the end of our call, we believed that now was our moment, despite the risk, the possibility of failure, and the many unknowns. **Someday was today.**

We had clarity about what we wanted and the need for what we could offer, and that made being bold and taking action easier. That was ten years ago, and we have relied on that same process of finding clarity, being bold, and taking action to build and grow our company, The Fast Forward Group. Now we help thousands of people achieve success and happiness year after year.

We respect so many of the books designed to help us all be more effective, productive, healthier, and happier, but most don't help readers answer "What?" and "Why?" *What* do *you* want your life to look like? *Why* make the effort to go for something different? The answer might *seem* obvious, but for many of us, it isn't. Like Avery, **we can be so immersed in our present circumstances and in the stories we tell about them, we can't lift our heads and gain perspective.** We may think we know what we want and believe we're working toward it, but often we're working toward goals we "should" want or that other people want for us. Or we're focused on the things we're lacking rather than what would bring us joy and fulfillment.

When we discover an idea or a goal that's exciting, we tend to hold back from going for it, as Lisa was tempted to do. We believe the risks are too great. We see hurdles that aren't actually there and, like Avery, we don't have a strong belief in our ability to make change happen—so we don't take action.

When you have clarity—about what you want *and* about what's actually keeping you from it—it's easier to be bold and focus on specific, strategic actions that create momentum. **You'll need clarity, a willingness to be bold, and the motivation to take action to leverage your power to create the life you want.** With each Power Principle, we'll help you achieve all three.

HOW TO GET THE MOST OUT OF THIS BOOK—AND YOUR LIFE

We want to get a simple truth out of the way before we go any further. **Creating meaningful change in your life often means getting uncomfortable.** It means being an active participant. It means taking 100 percent responsibility for the things you *can* control—your behaviors, your perspective, your time, and how you react to and influence others. It means growth in your mindset and in your capabilities, and growth is usually uncomfortable.

Consequently, this is not a passive, big-think, rah-rah book. We'll be sharing important ideas and research, but we'll also be sharing exercises in *every* chapter. These are the same exercises we've used with over a hundred thousand people around the world. We know they are the fast-track to creating the life you want because we've seen it happen again and again. Even people who've been through other personal or leadership development programs have said that the Fast Forward program transformed their life—because it helped them understand the power they always had to do so.

If you're reading the ebook or listening to the audiobook, consider going to our website, https://fastforwardgroup.net/book, and downloading the accompanying workbook from the book page. It contains all of the exercises. We think it's most effective to do the exercises as you go, but we know that's not always possible. You might make your way through parts of the book, or even the whole thing, and then go back and work on the exercises later.

It's important to **write your answers down** because the act of writing shifts how we think about the ideas, stories, and feelings we've written. It creates more clarity. Sometimes, we're going to ask you to share your answers with people in your life. Again, this is important. Saying things out loud also changes how we think about them. What's most important is to be vulnerable, be honest, and work through the discomfort, because the key to success and happiness is getting comfortable with being uncomfortable.

That's what we'll help you do with each Power Principle.

With Power Principle 1, we'll help you connect with what you want most, think big, and declare a bold vision for one year from today. Creating a bold vision informed but not limited by your past or present can be tricky. Your brain will create obstacles. We'll help you overcome them by defining what success looks like *for you*—what *you* want to achieve, how *you* want to live, and how *you* want to show up for the people in your life. You'll tackle the limiting beliefs that have kept you from going for what you want. You'll connect with your childlike sense of possibility. And you'll discover how to enroll people in your vision, especially people who can offer support and accountability.

Through Power Principle 2, you'll learn how to identify the disempowering stories your brain creates—about others, about circumstances, and about yourself—and choose a more positive perspective that allows the future to be different than the past. It begins by differentiating between fact and perspective and recognizing the cost of believing the negative stories. We'll share our proven approach to choosing more empowering perspectives and putting them into action. This shift fuels your ability to overcome long-standing mental hurdles and move past the thinking that eats away at your confidence.

Power Principle 3 will help you discover how to become more than just a busy person with a to-do list. Instead of feeling like there is never enough time for the things you want, you'll discover how to have exactly enough and start taking ground immediately. The first step is acknowledging where in your life you're being reactive—unconsciously eating away at your own time, energy, and focus—rather than intentional. With that clarity, you can reverse engineer your bold vision into a 90-day action plan that helps you make progress with *manageable* actions and habits. We finish this section with simple, confidence-building strategies for saying no to things that pull you off track.

In Power Principle 4, we'll shift our focus to communication, which is key to accomplishing your bold vision. By becoming a more confident communicator, you'll be able to grow your influence and impact, encourage action to get more done, and enlist support for projects and ideas that are important to you. First, we'll help you discover how often you communicate like an observer "in the stands" rather than a participant "on the field," using action-centered language to aid progress. Then, we'll show you how to set a desired outcome and plan important conversations so that you're taking ground, one conversation and meeting at a time.

With Power Principle 5, we'll help you develop your curiosity muscle and expand what's possible in your life through the power of conscious listening. We'll begin by helping you understand what gets in the way of effective listening and what poor listening habits cost you in your relationships, knowledge, and impact. Then you can unleash your conscious listening to ignite collaboration and innovative thinking. We'll give you habits and strategies to be more present with people you care about, to deepen your relationships, and to help people solve their own problems—freeing you up to focus on your most important priorities.

Throughout the book, we'll share stories of people from all kinds of backgrounds and in all kinds of life situations who struggled to create the life they wanted. They often felt stuck, trapped, unfulfilled, or overwhelmed. **These stories are based on the stories of real people working through real challenges, gathered from our workshops and from interviews we conducted for this book.** In most cases, we've changed details (names, locations, industries, genders) to protect their anonymity. Occasionally, we've combined two similar stories to paint a more complete picture of how an idea or model plays out in real-world situations. And we'll share our own stories of struggling to overcome the hurdles we tackle in the book. You may notice that many of the people in our stories were uncomfortable as they worked through the process. But in the end, they were always happy they did.

Remember, you have the power to create the life you want, but that means doing the work, even when it's uncomfortable and even when you don't like it. We can't wait to hear what you accomplish.

YOUR FIRST EXERCISE

If you want to use the free accompanying workbook to capture your answers to all of the exercises in the book, you can find it at FastForwardGroup.net/book. Whether or not you use the workbook, take a minute now to think about the ideas we've shared in this chapter, especially the power you have to make your life what you want it to be. Then, answer this question:

What do you hope to get out of this book?

DECLARE A BOLD VISION

Throw Your Hat over the Wall

Chapter 2

THE MASSIVE VALUE OF BOLD VISIONS — AND HOW TO START

On the day that we met Jonah, his professional life was in turmoil.

He had worked in software sales for sixteen years, the past six with the same company. He was a respected team leader. He liked his manager and coworkers, and the organization invested in its employees. Sounds like a great situation, right? He had every reason to feel satisfied with and energized by his work.

Most days, he did not.

With every passing year, his work felt like more of a grind. He wasn't growing. He wasn't motivated by a promotion to the next obvious position, but he had to pretend he was so that he didn't get labeled as "lacks ambition." He rarely felt proud of what he had accomplished at the end of each month—with one exception.

For about four years, Jonah had been running training programs on sales skills, such as customer-focused communication. He had started small, working with new people on the team, but he soon recognized that even experienced team members could benefit. He got permission to develop more programs. After a couple of years, he asked if he could expand and include people from the corporate partnerships team.

The weeks he ran training programs were the most fulfilling weeks of the year. He couldn't wait for the next one. He loved developing the content, working to make it engaging, and learning about effective teaching strategies. It lit him up. He was so proud of the positive feedback he got from people who attended that he would read their comments to his wife. Over time, his coworkers started to ask, "Why aren't you doing this full time?"

In his mind, the answer was simple: *It's not possible.*

He didn't have any background in training and development, and changing careers would mean starting at the bottom. His family couldn't afford that. His company had a small training and development team, but no role for an internal sales or communications trainer.

About a week before we met Jonah, one of the company's biggest products suffered a security breach, putting customer data at risk. Clients were canceling their subscriptions, and Jonah's team lost 25 percent of their revenue almost overnight. Perhaps they could have reversed the trend, but two people were about to begin their parental leave and another seemed to have one foot out the door. Jonah wasn't sure how to solve any of this. Worse, he was totally unmotivated to try.

At our Fast Forward workshop the next week, we asked Jonah (and a group of his colleagues) to fast-forward one year and describe what extraordinary success looked like. One idea came through loud and clear: *I'm no longer in sales. I train and develop people, and I love it.*

It was a **bold vision.** It was a big change from where he was in his career, and he didn't know how to make it happen. It felt risky and uncomfortable, and he thought there was a good chance it wouldn't happen. It would require him to grow and change. It would require the support of his family and his professional network. For all those reasons, he hadn't declared that vision or goal at any point in the four years since discovering his professional passion.

Can you relate to Jonah's experience? For instance,

- Have you ever stayed in a job you didn't like because you didn't think a better option was possible for you?
- Have you ever stayed in a relationship that was comfortable but that you knew wasn't going anywhere?
- Have you ever let your personal passions or your health slide off your priority list?

What does staying safe and comfortable cost you?

Fulfillment? Motivation? Happiness? Despite the costs, most of us choose to stick with the status quo, even when we aren't all that happy with it. Going for something bigger or different, especially when the path to get there isn't obvious, triggers the brain's risk-avoidance strategies. Our focus shifts to all the things we might lose and the ways we might fail. **Playing it safe is a habit that isn't easy to break.**

While it's not our usual approach to life, it's likely that at some point *you have* declared and achieved a bold vision. You took a leap, told the world what you wanted, and then went to work making it happen. Maybe you moved cities, took a job that you weren't sure you were ready for, or started your own company. Maybe you asked somebody to marry you, ran a marathon, or bought a new house. Even though you've set and achieved a big goal in the past, it's not easy to keep doing it or to do it consistently, year after year. The moments when you played big and didn't succeed can dominate your thinking, and the longer you stay in a situation, the more attached you become to what you have rather than what you could gain.

In this chapter, we're going to inspire you to overcome these tendencies by exploring the massive benefits of declaring a bold vision. A bold vision expands what's possible in the future, but it also dramatically changes your life in the present. We'll help you build confidence in your ability to achieve something bigger and better by addressing the first hurdle—your own limiting beliefs. We'll explore the brain science behind *why* we stick with the status quo. In the next chapter, we'll take you step by step through our unique bold vision exercise, helping you dream in color about your whole life. Your power to *change* the future begins with a compelling vision of the future, and **the most inspiring visions are those that are informed *but not limited by* our past and present.** That's why we're starting with your mindset.

That's where Jonah had to start. He had to shift his thinking about what his future could look like. He was so lit up by his bold vision, the first person he shared it with was *his boss*. After she recovered from the shock, they began to discuss how she could help. Her support helped him believe it might be possible. Month by month, Jonah figured out what it would take, found a team he wanted to join, and prepared his family for the big change (which included a drop in salary while he worked his way up). He didn't make the transition in a year, but that was okay. He was motivated again, and it felt great to be honest with himself and his colleagues about his aspirations—no more pretending. This all happened about seven years ago. Today, Jonah is the national director of training and development for his company, and he is happy, fulfilled, and growing.

That is what a bold vision realized can look like.

YOUR ACTIONS IN THE PRESENT ARE DIRECTLY CORRELATED TO THE FUTURE YOU BELIEVE IS POSSIBLE

In 1961, the Irish author Frank O'Connor published *An Only Child*, his memoir of growing up in poverty and becoming a writer. Houses and apartments were too small to gather inside, and so he spent his time outside, roaming the countryside with his schoolmates. "When as kids we came to an orchard wall that seemed too high to climb," he wrote, "we took off our caps and tossed them over the wall, and then we had no choice but to follow them."[1]

>>

When we ask people to throw their hats over the wall, this is what we mean: Give yourself something so compelling to play for, you don't have a choice but to go for it.

>>

When Frank O'Connor was a boy, he was playing for adventure—and to avoid having to tell his parents, who had no money, that he had lost his only cap. But at fourteen, with only a limited education, he began to realize a much more compelling vision. He wanted to be a writer. After months of studying on his own, he wrote his first serious essay on language and culture and then stood up at a meeting of the Gaelic League and read it to an audience of adults. "All that did matter was the act of faith," he wrote about that moment, "the hope that somehow, somewhere I would be able to prove that I was neither mad nor a good-for-nothing; because now I realized that whatever it might cost me, there was no turning back . . . I had tossed my cap over the wall of life, and I knew I must follow it, wherever it had fallen."

That act of faith can be hard, especially when we don't know how or when we'll achieve our goal. What most people don't realize, though, is that having a bold vision creates *immediate* benefits, because your actions in the present are correlated to the future you see as possible. What do we mean by that? The moment-by-moment choices you make about what to do, what not to do, how to show up, where to devote your time and energy, and more are informed by the future you're trying to create. The clearer you are about what you're playing for, the more empowered you are to make choices that align with your vision of the future *and* that steadily improve your life *now*.

Getting Creative and Solving Problems

As soon as you've thrown your hat over the wall, your brain will go to work trying to figure out how to follow it. Even when you aren't consciously thinking about it, your subconscious is working it out.

Peter Senge, systems scientist, MIT Sloan School of Management lecturer, and expert on high-performance organizations and people, calls this "creative tension." He explained that the source of creative tension is the difference between our current reality and our vision—between this side of the wall and the other. "It's not what the vision is, it's what the vision does," he wrote, meaning that when something you envision for your future lights you up just thinking about it—whatever that thing is—you will confidently and creatively find the necessary steps to make it happen.[2] You will change your current reality to move it closer and closer to your vision. As your brain tries to figure out how to get you over the wall, you start overcoming small obstacles, shifting your behavior, clearing out the clutter, making progress. You find yourself solving problems that previously seemed impossible.

Again, at some point in your life, you've done this. You looked out into the future and saw something so compelling that you got creative, resourceful, and intentional until you figured it out. You trained for (and ran) a marathon, figuring out week by week how to be more disciplined and healthier. You moved to a new city and built a life there, and along the way you figured out how to meet people with shared interests or how to pursue new interests so that you could build a community. You applied to an MBA program, got in, and then figured out how to stick with it while keeping your day job. What fueled you between the time you said, "I'm doing this" and the time you made it happen? Excitement about the future, yes, but also more joy and fulfillment in the present as you solved problems, eliminated small and large frustrations, and accomplished goals.

Clarity About What Matters

Wouldn't it be great if your decisions about where and how to spend your time, your money, and your energy were more purposeful? To weed out the unimportant, you need clarity on what *is* important. That's what a bold vision can offer.

One of our clients, Terrell, realized that benefit early in his work with Wendy. They were on a coaching call when he shared some great news. "My boss came to me yesterday and encouraged me to apply for an open leadership position."

"Wow, that's great! It must feel good to know he's got such confidence in you."

"Yes, but I've got two young kids," he said. "Taking on a bigger role right now would be too hard. I would have to travel. My husband's career is taking off, too." The stability and predictability of Terrell's job had worked for him for some time, but he told us he felt he was starting to stagnate. "The role would help me grow, but I don't see how to make it happen." Wendy kept nudging him, but he kept bringing up all of his commitments outside of work.

"Okay, but what *could* it look like?"

Sparking Terrell's imagination helped him take a step back from the day-to-day minutia, look at his life as a whole, and ask himself, *What would have to change for me to take this on?* And that question led to an even more important one: *What commitments* actually *matter to me and to my family?* As he listed tasks and responsibilities and things he took on at home or at his kids' school, it became clear that he was saying yes to things that didn't matter to him, that didn't excite him, and that probably didn't matter to his family. He left the call with a goal: find out what *did* matter. When he asked, he found out that they didn't care if he chaperoned field trips or did the grocery shopping or even whether he was there for dinner every night. What they did appreciate was him being there on the weekends for fun family time and at the end of the day to read with the kids, and that he continued his role as assistant coach of their soccer team. His husband, Michael, said that with a little extra money, they could hire somebody to mow the lawn and do some of the regular maintenance on the house that Terrell usually handled.

With his priorities clear, Terrell started to believe he could make the new role work. The next week, he threw his hat over the wall and applied for the new position. He blocked out a couple of afternoons for coaching time and let go of all the stuff that neither he nor his family cared about. In the end, he got the job. He felt energized by his work again *and* felt successful as a parent and partner.

Throwing your hat over the wall helps you recognize the power you already have to choose your priorities and take control of your life.

After crafting a bold vision, most of our participants find that they're *accomplishing* more and *doing* less. They feel confident and intentional in their choices, rather than reactive and out of control (we'll dive into how to do this in Power Principle 3). You can achieve the same when you have a bold vision that becomes your north star.

WHY IS GOING FOR WHAT YOU WANT SO HARD?

We viscerally understand that there's power in declaring a bold vision. If it can be so compelling, inspiring, and transforming, why is it so hard?

We're intentional about using the word *declare* because it's a term people don't like to use. It's uncomfortable. **What gets in the way? Fear of failing, of not being able to get over the wall, and of everything that might mean.** This is especially true for our boldest visions—because often we don't know how to make them happen. As enticing as they are, they're riskier. We believe we'll be judged, we'll lose credibility, we'll look foolish. What does it say about us or our potential if we fail at a goal we set? That risk might feel too great.

The Nobel-prize-winning economist Daniel Kahneman and his colleague Amos Tversky spent years trying to understand how we deal with risk and how it affects our decisions. What they found and captured in their well-known prospect theory is that the brain gives more decision-making weight to avoiding loss than it does to gaining something of the same or even greater value. We'll choose to avoid losing $100 over taking a risk to win $120.[3]

Other "cognitive biases," a term coined by Kahneman and Tversky, work against us, too. One is called status quo bias. Researchers have proven over and over that when we have the option, we prefer to stick with the status quo.[4] As evolutionary psychologists have explained, our safety once depended on this kind of risk or loss avoidance. When early civilizations lived on the edge of survival, with barely enough food and shelter, losing even a little could mean the end. Because of this, the human brain evolved to spend a lot of time scanning for potential threats and avoiding them. It likes certainty and predictability. It likes to *know* what's going to happen next. Even today, this keeps us safe—by predicting whether we'll be able to get across the street before that car gets to the crosswalk, for instance. But in a work setting, when we're choosing between staying where we are or going for something that we aren't sure how to (or if) we'll achieve, which option will be our default?

That's just how we're wired as human beings. **Most of us are good at sticking with the status quo, even when it doesn't serve us.** Often, we don't take the time to figure out what it is we *do* want or what might be possible if we went for it. We avoid *even thinking* about the risk of trying. Let's say that you take the leap and declare a bold vision—and don't make it. So what? You'll learn, you'll grow, and you'll give yourself something to feel proud of, even if it wasn't the exact outcome you were going for.

Just by trying, you'll make positive change happen in your life. You'll end up achieving more than you would have if you *hadn't* gone for it.

Yes, some failures come with outsized repercussions, but most of the time, our catastrophizing is unwarranted. We're also not suggesting that you put *everything* on the line. We're encouraging you to look at your whole life and be bold in a way that helps you achieve the life you want for the coming year. (In the next chapter, we'll dive into what we mean by "bold.")

Any of us can briefly lose hope when we fail (more on this in a minute), but **researchers have found that failing to achieve a goal doesn't have a significant negative impact on our happiness.**[5] What matters more is having a goal to begin with. People who have goals are generally happier than people who don't. Without them, it feels like our future is in the control of other people and circumstances—because it is.

GETTING OUT OF YOUR OWN WAY: LIMITING BELIEFS

When Lisa's son, John, was nine, he said, "Mom, I'm not sure what I want to be when I grow up because I'm so good at everything!" Now, maybe that level of belief wasn't realistic, but because of it, he threw himself into things with energy and enthusiasm, certain that he could achieve anything he wanted.

Can you remember the last time you had that much confidence in the possibilities of your future—the last time it felt wide open to you? It might have been when you were a kid. But then you accumulated experiences, and they started to shape your view of the future and your beliefs about what's possible. Martin Seligman, the "father of positive psychology," has explained that we experience feelings of helplessness and lack of control when we fail.[6] When we have more of those experiences, that feeling can become ingrained in our thinking, a state he calls "learned helplessness." **Less-than-positive events from our past "teach" us that some things are simply out of reach or that some situations can't be changed. It's usually not true, but the brain processes it like it *is* true.**

The problem gets compounded because we remember negative experiences far better than positive ones. As psychologist Rick Hanson wrote about the brain's memory storage, "Your brain is like Velcro for negative experiences and Teflon for positive ones—even though most of your experiences are probably neutral or positive."[7] Researchers have used MRI technology to show that the regions of our brains associated with memory light up when we are processing negative events.[8] The more negative the experience, the more vividly we remember it, especially the details most associated with our negative emotions, like fear, shame, or disappointment.

The bottom line is that **you're more likely to accurately and vividly remember those times when you tried and failed than those times when you tried and succeeded.** Again, the brain operates this way for a reason: survival. If we forget and then repeat experiences that were painful or frightening, we're probably not going to be around very long. This kind of thinking might keep us physically safe—by teaching us that we're somewhat helpless against fire and great white sharks, and that we should avoid them—but we can't pick and choose where we apply it.

It doesn't help us *thrive*.

We go through life dragging the past along with us, like luggage filled with all of our confidence-busting moments. It weighs us down and slows our progress. It makes it difficult to freely imagine something substantially different from how things are right now. It creates limiting beliefs about what's possible.

Our limiting beliefs can keep us from playing big in life.

They can keep us stuck. Lots of people have aspirations they aren't even willing to name because they're resigned to them never happening. Just look at Jonah's story. What did he believe about doing the work he loved? It wasn't possible. That wasn't true, but he believed it was. And because of that, he didn't do the things necessary in the present to make it happen—until we helped him move to overcome his limiting beliefs.

For other people, especially those who are "firsts" or who have overcome major hurdles to get where they are, their limiting beliefs can create insecurities about their success. As one participant, Aliyah, told us, "I have a huge amount of fear of ending up back where I started. It wasn't easy to get where I am now. I was the first in my family to graduate from college, to move away from where I grew up, to make the kind of money I do. Sometimes I feel like one wrong move, and I'll be back at square one." This kind of thinking can make people prioritize work over personal health and well-being.

A vision built on bold declarations requires confidence that the future can look different than the present or the past. It requires belief in your possibilities. The good news is that with a bit of effort, you can override the negative programming. You can combat your limiting beliefs by focusing on positive, optimistic, hopeful thoughts and stories. We'll go deeper on how to do this in Power Principle 2, but the first step is to acknowledge where you're getting in your own way—where you're limiting your future based on what has happened in the past or where you are in the present. If you don't overcome your limiting beliefs, you'll keep maintaining the status quo or keep playing small, turning those beliefs into self-fulfilling prophecies. Let's make sure that's not happening for you.

Acknowledging Limiting Beliefs — and Imagining Something Different

We hold limiting beliefs about ourselves, about others, and about circumstances. Read through the following examples and see if any feel familiar.

Limiting Beliefs About Ourselves
- I'm not good with conflict.
- I'm not comfortable with large groups.
- I'm not a strong storyteller/presenter.
- If I don't respond immediately, people will think I'm not on top of things.
- I'm not smart/funny/creative/strategic enough.
- I'm a bad parent/child/friend/sibling.

- I have no discipline.
- I am bad with details/disorganized.

Limiting Beliefs About Others

- I can't count on people/it's easier to do it myself.
- People are selfish.
- My manager doesn't appreciate me.
- That team is a bottleneck.
- My partner does nothing, and I have to do everything.
- My kids are spoiled and don't appreciate me.

Limiting Beliefs About Circumstances

- It's hard to be healthy with the demands of my job.
- It's tough to succeed at both a career and a personal life.
- Moving up at my company requires sacrifice.
- That would never work here.
- There are not enough hours in the day.
- It's very political here.
- It's hard to make new friends at my age.
- It's too hard to meet someone in this city.

We're sure you can relate to one or more of these examples—and that's good. Raising your consciousness of your *own* limiting beliefs is an important step in being able to challenge them! The next exercise is our limiting beliefs exercise. Write out your answers to the three questions we've shared. The act of writing will help you gain clarity.

Try to be clear and specific, especially with the last question. **You're starting to envision a different future and coming up with new language you can use to design it.** If you can, find somebody to share it with. Saying your limiting belief out loud often helps shed some of the significance and drama, or helps you see the fallacy behind it. Once you finish the exercise, you'll probably feel lighter.

EXERCISE: ACKNOWLEDGING YOUR LIMITING BELIEFS

Spend a few minutes thinking about your strongest limiting beliefs, those that hold you back from taking risks or going for what you want in both big and small ways. Choose the one that has the most heat, the most negative emotion associated with it, or that comes up most often. Now, **write down your answers** to the following questions.

1. What is the limiting belief?
    Example: I can't count on people, so I have to do everything myself.

2. How does it limit you? What is the cost of this belief in your life?
    Example: My bandwidth is constrained because I'm doing everything myself. I feel overwhelmed, exhausted, and resentful. I get less accomplished, and I'm not empowering other people to accomplish more. I'm not growing and they're not growing.

3. Fast-forward one year from today: You have let this belief go and it has no effect on your life anymore. (This will require using your imagination; resist the temptation to say to yourself, "That's not possible.") What's different? What's now possible? How do you feel? Write your answer as if it has already happened.
    Example: I am delegating tasks, which allows me to focus on what's most important at work and home. I am not working on weekends. My team at work is growing and challenged. My

spouse is sharing the cooking and errands. I feel calm when I go to sleep at night.

You can download the workbook, which contains all exercises in the book, at FastForwardGroup.net/Book.

Believing that the future can look different from the past or the present takes courage and tenacity, but any of us can take this leap of faith. When we ask people what parts of our work together had the greatest impact on their life, they almost always say it was throwing their hat over the wall. It was getting comfortable being uncomfortable and declaring a bold vision. In the next chapter, we'll help you do exactly that, in a way that gives you the best possible shot at succeeding.

Chapter 3

IMAGINE THE POSSIBILITIES JUST ONE YEAR FROM TODAY

Fast-forward one year from today. What does extraordinary success look like in your *whole* life?

That is the provocative question at the core of the bold vision exercise that we're about to share with you. More than a hundred thousand people have used this exercise to accomplish the extraordinary feat of creating the personal *and* professional life they want. Working through it required them to challenge their limiting beliefs so that they could paint a vivid and compelling picture of the near future. As a result, they found inspiration, clarity, and focus.

The best example we've seen of declaring a bold vision came from US President John F. Kennedy. In 1962, he delivered a speech at Rice University announcing that we would put a man on the moon before the decade was out. Kennedy knew the public and other leaders weren't sold on the idea. It seemed far-fetched, too expensive, and like a distraction from the Cold War. He countered by painting a shining picture of what success *could* look like, addressing the mental hurdles we all face when we try to think big and envision something we don't know how to accomplish:

> *We choose to go to the moon in this decade and do the other things, not because they are easy, but because they are hard, because that goal will serve to organize and measure the best of our energies and skills, because that challenge is one that we are willing to accept, one we are unwilling to postpone, and one which we intend to win.*
>
> . . .
>
> *[W]e shall send to the moon, 240,000 miles away from the control station in Houston, a giant rocket more than 300 feet tall, the length of this football field, made of new metal alloys, some of which have not yet been invented, capable of standing heat and stresses several times more than have ever been experienced, fitted together with a precision better than the finest watch, carrying all the equipment needed for propulsion, guidance, control, communications, food, and survival, on an untried mission, to an unknown celestial body, and then return it safely to earth, re-entering the atmosphere at speeds of over 25,000 miles per hour, causing heat about half that of the temperature of the sun — almost as hot as it is here today — and do all this, and do it right, and do it first before this decade is out — then we must be bold.*

Exciting, right? Compelling visions that pull us forward to a better future have to overcome the obstacles created by our brains' fear of failure, loss avoidance tendency, and negativity bias. Kennedy and his speech writers understood that. Your vision can be just as powerful, just as bold. It all begins with your language.

>>

**Language creates reality. The belief that
something is possible starts and is continuously
reaffirmed in our language.**

>>

You may have used other goal-setting models in the past and they may have worked for you. But a powerful vision that creates a compelling guide to action has distinct characteristics, and we've woven them into our exercise. In this chapter, we'll guide you through our proven process of crafting a vision that has a deep impact on your life, starting with how to get into the right mindset and give your brain what it needs to stay motivated.

A VISION THAT MOTIVATES US TO ACT

To create a vision that motivates us and lights us up, we have to know what we authentically want, and we have to craft it in a way that makes it easier for us to achieve. Look back at the Kennedy speech. What stands out for you about his language? Here's what most people notice when we share the video in our programs:

- It's highly specific, with vivid details and measurable outcomes.
- It has a clear deadline (within the next seven years).
- Kennedy freely acknowledged that they didn't know how they were going to accomplish it, that they hadn't even invented materials or technology they would need. They had problems to solve to reach the goal.

In their book *Switch*, Chip and Dan Heath described how those characteristics help engage the two ways the brain responds to ideas—emotionally and logically. Daniel Kahneman calls them System 1 and System 2. A compelling vision should be inspiring and engaging for your emotional, reactive mind. It should also be clear, specific, and measurable to give your analytical, rational, problem-solving mind something to work on. You need both systems or ways of thinking aligned to move forward. When the two aren't on the same page, change is difficult.

This is why our vision process is based on one year. One year is long enough to make big things happen and set exciting goals that are emotionally engaging. It's also a near enough deadline to give the analytical, planning part of your brain a reason to start figuring out how to get there *now* rather than *eventually*. You can immediately start tracking your progress, and that builds your confidence.

Let's look at more ways our vision exercise strikes a balance between engaging the head and heart.

What Do We Mean by "Bold"?

In the same way people shy away from the word "declare," they also often aren't that comfortable with the word "bold." It sounds risky. So before we ask you to be bold, we'll explain what we mean and what a difference it makes.

Below is a continuum. On one end are goals that would be highly predictable—meaning you can feel almost certain you'll achieve them. On the other end are goals that would be pure fantasy. If Lisa set a vision to be punctual, that would be highly predictable because she's almost always on time already. What would be the point? If she set a goal to become fluent in German and Mandarin in the next year, that would be pure fantasy. There would be no way to accomplish it. If your vision is made up entirely of *overly* predictable goals, it will require almost no growth. It would be comfortable and hold you within the status quo, which comes with a high cost of stagnation and demotivation because it isn't exciting. Fantastical goals don't motivate you or lead to growth, either, because you give up on them almost immediately. A vision that sits at either end of the spectrum is unlikely to help you achieve positive change in your behaviors, choices, or life.

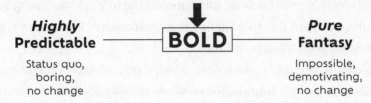

We recommend you aim for the center for many of the goals you include in your vision. That said, your vision should also include elements that are somewhat predictable but still *important*. You don't want to lose sight of them as you work toward the bolder elements of your vision, which require growth and change. For instance, if you're currently making progress on a health goal and have already cemented some healthy habits, great. You'll probably still mention them in your vision because you don't want those habits to fall by the wayside as you work on bolder goals.

The bold elements of your vision can make you feel uncomfortable, but being uncomfortable is where the magic happens. It's where creative energy and innovation come from. It's a sign that you'll need to overcome hurdles and behaviors holding you back—and that's a good thing! Bold visions often involve people or factors outside of your control, which increases the feeling of risk.

―――――――――――― ≫ ――――――――――――

You don't need to know how to achieve your bold goals. Focusing on "how," on predictability, or on certainty holds people back from dreaming in color.

―――――――――――― ≫ ――――――――――――

You'll likely feel both uncomfortable *and* energized, with butterflies in your stomach, when you finish our vision exercise. It's like the first day in a new job, or the first time you rode a bike. Every time you do the exercise, though, you'll get more comfortable setting bold outcomes that you aren't sure how to accomplish. You'll get more comfortable being uncomfortable.

We want to make an important point here. A bold vision does not have to mean doing "more." We aren't leading you toward a life that is busier, more chaotic, or more stressful. A compelling vision should do the opposite. When Wendy's children were younger, one of her boldest aspirations was to do less—to spend more time sitting on the floor playing with them instead of constantly running from thing to thing. Your vision should bring you clarity and help you prioritize.

As you work through the questions, ask yourself, **"Why is this important?" "What difference will this make?"** and **"What is uncomfortable about this outcome?"** If the answer to the third question is "nothing," you aren't being bold enough.

Start with the Finish

In their book *The Art of Possibility*, Rosamund Stone Zander and Benjamin Zander describe a technique that Ben used with his students at the New England Conservatory of Music. He wanted to free students from the anxiety of performing well in his class so they could focus on performing creatively and without limits as musicians. So on the first day of class, he told them that they would all be getting As. And then he gave them his one requirement:

> *"You must write me a letter dated next May, which begins with the words, 'Dear Mr. Zander, I got my A because . . . ;' and in this letter you are to tell, in as much detail as you can, the story of what will have happened to you by next May that is in line with this extraordinary grade." In writing their letters, I say to them, they are to place themselves in the future, looking back, and to report on all the insights they acquired and the milestones they attained during the year as if those accomplishments were already in the past . . . I tell them, "I am especially interested in the person you will have become by next May. I am interested in the attitude, feelings, and worldview of that person who will have done all she wished to do or become everything he wanted to be."*[1]

We want you to do the same. We want you to "begin with the end in mind," to quote Stephen R. Covey, author of *The 7 Habits of Highly Effective People*.[2] Fast-forward one year from today. It's been an extraordinarily successful year. Imagine you're talking with a good friend about the important, meaningful goals you achieved. Visualize yourself in that future moment, including how you feel, think, and behave. Write your vision as if you're in that future moment, using present or past tense to indicate that your goals have happened or are happening.

Be Specific and Vivid in Your Answers

We were working with a group of executives on bold outcomes in their professional lives. One man, Travis, wrote, "We improved our 'difficult' relationship with the product development team." What does that mean? we asked. How would you know if you were succeeding? It was too vague to be motivating or build belief or confidence.

Vague goals are more comfortable because they give us wiggle room. That also makes them disempowering and unmotivating. You can't know when or if you "become a better manager" or "spend more time with my son." You can't measure *better* or *more* or *improved*. They aren't vivid enough to be emotionally compelling and they aren't specific enough to give your analytical brain something to creatively "solve." Yet, these are the kinds of goals most of us set.

When answering the questions, ask yourself, **"How will I know this is happening?"** and **"How will things be different when I achieve this?"** When it makes sense, include metrics that would help you measure success. Use emotionally vivid language to paint an inspiring picture, and capture how you feel. What is deeply compelling about the vision, for both your head and heart?

When we shared those prompts, Travis reworked his professional outcomes: "Collaborating with the product development team, we launched a new product that generated $1 million in revenue. I have a friendly, productive relationship with their leader, and we are transparent about our goals." As soon as he shared it with us, his creative, analytical brain went to work, and he listed four or five obstacles that would have to be overcome and actions he could take to make that possible.

Success in Your Whole Life

A vision that only addresses one aspect of life is a recipe for stress and possible failure. For instance, going for a big promotion without thinking about how to also achieve what you want personally feeds the idea that you have to make trade-offs. That's not true! You don't have to make sacrifices in your personal life to achieve what you want in your professional life, or vice versa.

The most effective visions encompass our whole lives — all the things we care about, all the things we want deeply, all the things that light us up.

A powerful vision will show you a path to the kind of happiness, peace, and fulfillment that can't be found in compartments. Bold moves often require change and growth in multiple aspects of your life. As you work through the questions, ask, "What impact does this have *on my life as a whole*?"

Give yourself a vision so clear and compelling to play for, you don't have a choice but to go for it. Throw your hat over the wall, and in doing so, take back the power to create the life you want.

BOLD VISION EXERCISE

As you answer each of the seven vision questions in the following pages, deepen your answers by asking

- What about this is uncomfortable or unpredictable? Why?
- Have I written my answer as if it's already happened or is happening, using the past or present tense?
- What about this is important?
- What difference will it make when this happens?
- How will I know that it happened or if I'm making progress?

Question 1: What are you known for?

Question 2: What were your professional (business and career) outcomes?

Question 3: How would you describe the culture of your team or company?

Question 4: What were your personal outcomes?

Question 5: How did you grow and improve?

Question 6: What is your outlook on life?

Question 7: How would you describe the quality of your important relationships?

1. WHAT ARE YOU KNOWN FOR?

We start with this question because very few of us spend time in our lives thinking about it. Most of us aren't conscious of how we're showing up or aren't setting intentions for how we want to show up.

Lisa: Years ago, I was a senior executive at a large corporation and had two young children. I was constantly in motion, mentally and physically, reacting to the next thing I needed to do or solve.

People on my team would literally follow me down the hall to get my attention.

Right after my second maternity leave, I was given the opportunity to attend a leadership development program where the first exercise was to write my own eulogy. I considered dropping out, but the allure of a hotel room all to myself for two nights compelled me to move ahead. They suggested we interview the people who knew us well and ask, "What am I known for?" This was one of the most confronting experiences of my life, and a serious wake-up call. Everybody said the same thing: I was known for being *really busy*. It shouldn't have been a surprise. When people asked me how I was, I said, "I'm really busy."

This was a moment of absolute clarity. In my interviews, I discovered how this way of being negatively affected the people in my life. My team didn't feel heard. They thought I was impatient and didn't delegate appropriately. My family was not getting the attention they deserved. My friends had simply stopped inviting me to things, because they were sure that the answer would be no.

I could have rationalized why this was the case—demanding job, travel, long commute, two young children—but I was not okay with being known for being really busy. So I set an intention and declared a bold vision. In my eulogy, I wrote, "Lisa was calm and present. She made time for people she cared about—her family and her friends. She was a motivating leader who coached people to grow in their careers and lives." At the time, this was *beyond* a bold vision. It was borderline fantasy—but why play small? I chose to play big and set out to make it happen. When I told my husband, Sean, he was skeptical—"We'll see," he said—but I was determined.

The first thing I did was to stop saying, "I'm really busy" when people asked me how I was. Instead, I would say, "I'm in demand" or "I'm overly fulfilled." I spent more time sitting on the couch with my family, daily, to overcome my relentless focus on my to-do list and to show up as an engaged and loving mom and partner. I talked slower and I walked slower. I made eye contact. When people talked to me at work or at home, I listened attentively and shut out distractions.

I saw fast results, which built my confidence that I could change and my belief in the vision. After some time passed, I reinterviewed the people in my life, and I was so proud and grateful when people shared that they felt heard and connected with me and appreciated "the new Lisa." Being known as "calm and present" is still in my vision decades later . . . and I am still practicing. If I have a bad day, I recommit—and I have many supporters around me who will let me know when I'm off track!

Declaring a bold vision helps you stop living in reaction to the world around you. It helps you consider how to align your behavior with your values. With some reflection and intention, you can take control over how you are showing up. As you work on your answer to this question, remember to go deep and describe why these things are meaningful to you and others and how they make you feel.

"I AM KNOWN FOR" EXAMPLES

- *I am known as an inspiring leader who cares about people.* My team turns to me for mentorship and guidance and feels safe speaking up. Together, we achieve big goals without burning out.
- *I am known for giving the benefit of the doubt.* I assume people have good intentions and are giving their best. I trust people to treat me fairly, and they trust me to do the same.
- *I am known for speaking up and taking a stand on issues that are important to me.* People respect me for sharing my perspective in a clear and respectful

way that generates productive dialogue. I feel like I'm making a difference.

- *I am known for empowering people to learn and grow.* My kids are becoming responsible and independent, and the people on my team are excited to take on the tasks I delegate. I feel in control of my time.

2. WHAT WERE YOUR PROFESSIONAL OUTCOMES (BUSINESS AND CAREER)?

This is a good spot to raise an important cautionary point: **Your vision is not an exhaustive to-do list.** It doesn't have to include all the big and small things you think you need to accomplish. Remember, the overriding question is: What does extraordinary success look like for you? In your professional life, what would light you up? What would you feel *so* proud to accomplish? Most people include three or four big bets for the year. What would make coming to work every day exciting? Remember Jonah's story at the start of chapter two: His bold vision was to leave his sixteen-year career in sales and do something dramatically different. That level of change isn't usually necessary for people to feel energized at work, but if it is, don't hold back.

This is often the question where people tend to play it safe, stay comfortable, or write answers that are either vague or based on what other people want. It's an area of life where fear and limiting beliefs, especially about circumstances and the people we work with or for, can be strong. Remember, if you go for it and don't quite hit the mark, you'll accomplish more than you would have if you hadn't gone for it at all. You'll learn and grow from the experience.

Throw your hat over the wall and decide to make your career everything you want it to be, starting with this year. You have one life, and you won't get to do it over.

PROFESSIONAL OUTCOMES EXAMPLES

- I hit 110 percent of my quota. I brought in three new accounts worth $1 million each. I feel proud of the client relationships I have built and the way I collaborated with cross-functional teams to make this happen.
- I was promoted to director. I now lead a team of five people and I increased my compensation by 20 percent. I'm uncomfortable and growing!
- I have spoken at three conferences, and I feel confident and empowered speaking in front of groups. I've gotten positive feedback on my presentations and delivery.
- I managed two difficult, complex projects that left me feeling challenged and engaged. I communicated with my boss about my goal to become a senior analyst. I confidently ask for more responsibility when I feel I'm ready. I participate in two cross-department task forces that grow my understanding of our business and raise my profile with leaders.

3. HOW WOULD YOU DESCRIBE THE CULTURE OF YOUR TEAM OR COMPANY?

When we say culture, what do we mean? Culture defines how we do things: how we communicate and collaborate, how we treat each other, what behaviors we consider okay or not okay, what we celebrate, what kinds of stories we tell about other groups or teams. Because of this, the culture of the company or the team we work with has a profound impact on how we feel at work every day, as well as our overall well-being. As organizations like the American Psychological Association, Gallup, and many others have found, work is a *major* source of stress for most Americans. According to Jeffrey Pfeffer, Stanford professor of organizational behavior and author of *Dying for a Paycheck*, much of this stress stems from toxic, disrespectful, inefficient environments where people feel they have no control or input. "The workplace profoundly affects human health and mortality, and too many workplaces are harmful to people's health."[3]

You might think of culture as a leader's responsibility, and maybe you don't think of yourself as being in a leadership role because you don't carry that title. Or you might work for a large company and feel that the culture is completely out of your control. Many of us have a sense that culture is etched into tablets by people at the top and then handed down the mountain through layers of management. That's usually not how cultures evolve.

Let us tell you a story.

Jen was irritated during and after meetings with her colleagues and other teams. "When I'm talking, nobody makes eye contact with me," she said. "I feel insulted. It's like what I'm saying doesn't matter." People weren't looking at her because they were staring at their phones or laptops. Even worse, after meetings, people would come up and ask her questions that she had just answered! They were all busy and pressed for time, but by distracting themselves during important conversations, they were actually losing more time.

In her vision, Jen wrote, "Our meetings are efficient and effective. People eliminate distractions so that they can respectfully listen and offer great ideas." She shared her vision with colleagues who agreed that the problem needed to be solved. Together, they created agreements for meetings and enrolled more people in their vision. They got leaders on board. The discussion about meetings led to discussions about other communication challenges. As the months passed, they generated a big change in their workplace culture—all based on one person's bold vision.

You have the power to change your culture, too. You can be a role model in how you show up, how you behave, and in what you make okay or not okay. You can advocate for what you believe is right or important.

When you shift something that impacts your peace and well-being for eight to ten hours every day, the results can reverberate through your team, company, and life.

You can take a stand for the kind of culture you want.

CULTURE VISION EXAMPLES

- People feel it's safe to make mistakes and fail.
- We give each other clear, honest feedback and assume positive intent when we get it.
- We have fun and connect as people and teammates regularly.
- We value whole-life balance and use weekends to refuel and recharge.
- We value diverse perspectives and encourage new ideas; people feel heard regardless of their role, tenure, or cultural background.

4. WHAT WERE YOUR PERSONAL OUTCOMES?

Goal setting and achievement is woven into work life, even if we aren't always clear about our ambitions. What if you were to bring the same focus to your personal life? What if you were bold in your personal goals, too? For instance, when was the last time you committed to and rigorously pursued a goal for your health and well-being, a passion project, your finances, or something else important to you? If you're like most people, it's been a while. **We often deprioritize our personal lives, hoping things will improve by themselves or investing only whatever scraps of energy are left after a challenging day or week.**

Will wasn't even giving himself scraps. He was working at peak burn-out. Single and in his early thirties, he poured everything into his job leading a team at a fast-growth company. He didn't want to be single, but he rarely had time to meet new people or go out on dates, so nothing changed. He also wasn't proud of his health habits. Too many nights lately, he was going to the bar around the corner for a late-night drink or three with his coworkers before heading home to sleep for six hours—and then getting up to do it all again. He used to be fit, a runner for his college cross-country team. Now he wasn't sure he could run a mile without stopping.

Will had a good relationship with his boss, Jessica, which made it surprising to them both when he snapped at her one day. It had been an especially stressful week, and he was exhausted. "Okay," Jessica said. "Let's take a step back. I'm concerned about you. Other people on the team are leaving by 6:00 most nights, and I know you're here much later than that. Let me ask you this: What are you doing for you, outside of work?"

He didn't have an answer.

"Well, what's something you enjoy that you've stopped doing?"

Immediately, he thought of running, but quickly told Jessica that he didn't have time for it. Jessica pushed back and told him that she would support him coming in late one or two mornings a week if that's what it took. "Find a running club or a partner. I think you need this." (Side note: Wouldn't we all want to work for Jessica?)

Will set a goal to run three times a week. He began with short distances. In a month, he had worked his way up to a three-mile route. He joined a local running club, and at one of the meetings, he recognized a colleague from another department. They began to run together, too, becoming good friends. Because some of their runs were before work or early on the weekends, Will stopped going out for drinks most nights.

From there, it was a cascade. He became calmer, more clear-headed, and more positive. He also had more energy. When a woman he had dated in college moved to town and asked if he wanted to go to dinner, he knew how to carve out time for a relationship. And that's what he did. Today, they're happily married. When Will told us the story recently, he said, "It proved to me that if you're intentional about the things that matter and what you're going to do about them, then you start doing them. And it can affect the rest of your life." It helped that he had a supportive boss, but she didn't set the intention. She didn't do the work to build new habits.

What would extraordinary success look like in your personal life? What would it mean to you? Remember, this isn't a to-do list and it's not a list of "shoulds." It's a few carefully chosen outcomes that would make you feel excited, proud, or accomplished in a meaningful way. Choose wisely.

PERSONAL OUTCOMES EXAMPLES

- I have recommitted to karate and go to the dojo at least twice every week. I am a black belt, and I compete in the middleweight division. I feel strong and proud.
- I have thorough, written financial plans/goals. My partner and I don't argue about money. We talk about our plan, and we feel informed and confident about our financial future.
- I feel rested and have sustained energy and focus. I go to bed at roughly the same time and turn off tech an hour before. It has had a positive impact on my level of patience.
- I love my home and redone backyard. My family spends a lot of time outside now. Our home is a gathering place for friends and family.

5. HOW DID YOU GROW AND IMPROVE?

Most of us don't put any thought into how we want to grow and improve in the year ahead—even those of us who set goals or have an idea of where we're headed next. And yet, unlike many other things, **your growth and improvement is entirely within your control.** The effort we make to grow and how we grow is something we *can* own.

You might want to grow your knowledge, your skills, or your personal strengths and behaviors. Maybe you want to be a better communicator, become more knowledgeable about other departments in your company, or get better at delegating. The first step is identifying the one or two things that feel important to you or that could make a substantial difference in your whole life. For example, take Will from the story we shared in the last question. If he wanted to create a forcing function that would impact his life in a profound way, he might have written, "I create boundaries between my work life and personal life, making time for what's important in both. I use time management strategies that help me do this consistently."

Whatever it is, know that every year, you can be intentional about how you want to grow and improve, professionally and personally. You can end the year feeling accomplished and proud.

GROWTH AND IMPROVEMENT EXAMPLES

- I make decisions without second-guessing myself and feeling anxious for days or weeks afterward. I know that if a decision doesn't turn out as planned, I'll be able to adjust and get things back on track.
- I am confident and comfortable reading and talking about my company's financials and how they influence the executive team's decisions. It helps me connect my contributions to the company's bottom line.
- I say no to things at work and at home that aren't a good use of my time, and I do so without guilt. This frees me up to focus on the things that matter to me most. (We'll teach *you* how to do this in chapter ten!)

- I am resilient and use effective strategies to let go of things and bounce back from setbacks and losses.

6. WHAT IS YOUR OUTLOOK ON LIFE?

Every day we go through life with an outlook that influences how we see the world, how we interpret information, and how we react to circumstances and people. This is our outlook.

Most days, we don't think about it. We wake up, the sky is cloudy, we've already gotten a text from our boss, and we're in a crummy mood. The rest of the day, our outlook is dark and stormy. The next morning, the sun is shining, we read an inspiring article or positive email, and we're in a great mood. Our outlook is bright and positive.

Because we aren't intentional with our outlook, **many of us are also postponing our happiness because we believe it's tied to some future event or set of circumstances.** We might say to ourselves, "I will be so happy *when* I get promoted. *When* I meet someone, *then* I'll be happy. When I have more money, I'll be happy. When we have children, I'll be happy. When I retire, I'll be happy." And so on. In an article for TED, "joy-ologist" and designer Ingrid Fetell Lee describes the real danger of this mindset: "The habit of saying 'I'll be happy when . . .' keeps us waiting for life to happen to us instead of creating a life we want right now."[4]

What if you chose to be happy right now instead? We don't mean forcing positivity into days that are hard or denying negative emotions. We mean **giving yourself a touchstone that brings some intention to your outlook *most* days, because it is within your control.** (This is a really important concept and plays out in multiple ways in our lives, so we'll be discussing it further in chapters five and six.)

Think of the answer to this question like a mantra or a soundtrack to your day. You can choose to wake up every day and press play on happiness. What will your life sound like?

OUTLOOK EXAMPLES

- The best is yet to come.
- I appreciate what's working in my life.
- Good things will come out of this challenging time.
- Life is an adventure.
- I rise to the occasion.

7. HOW WOULD YOU DESCRIBE THE QUALITY OF YOUR IMPORTANT RELATIONSHIPS?

This is a meaty and emotional question, which is why we save it for last. In the words of author and psychotherapist Esther Perel, who has dedicated her life to studying the power of human connection, "The quality of our relationships determines the quality of our lives." That's why when we ask people, "How many of you have a relationship that you want to significantly improve?" almost everybody raises their hand.

We suggest you think about the quality of your relationships, and how they're affecting the quality of your life, in three areas.

The first is probably the most significant and lasting relationship that you will have in your lifetime: the relationship you have with yourself. Many of us could use improvement in this area, including how we talk to ourselves and how we talk *about* ourselves to other people. If you are taking yourself for granted, putting yourself last, or treating yourself poorly, you might decide that this is the year that you'll be kinder to yourself and take better care of yourself. In chapter seven, we'll share stories of somebody who worked to overcome their imposter syndrome and somebody who accepted that they deserved relationships that made them feel valued.

The second category of relationships is professional. You might choose to improve your relationship with your manager, or somebody who has an outsized impact on your success and happiness at work. Or you might focus on the relationship with someone on your team, an important partner, a peer, or a client. In Power Principle 5, we'll share stories of how listening and getting curious improved the relationship between a manager and his team and between an operations professional and her counterpart at another company.

The third category is personal. Consider your family, your friends, and people in your community, and how those relationships impact your happiness and well-being. Throughout the book, we'll tell many stories of how the Power Principles have improved personal relationships, including Wendy's relationship with her son, Ben; Lisa's relationship with her husband, Sean; and relationships between siblings.

You might have a relationship in your life that's "fine," but you would love it to be deeper and richer. You'd love to take the chance to get to know this person better, to feel more connected and comfortable with them, to feel you can be more authentic with them. Opportunities like these also have a place in your vision.

Many of us, though, have a relationship that creates feelings of frustration, sadness, or guilt. Some of us have personal or professional relationships that have been dysfunctional or strained for years, and we've become resigned to them being this way. We say, "This one's never getting any better" or "It's terrible, but there's nothing I can do about it." If you're thinking, *There's no way I'm putting that person in my vision*, instead say, *Wouldn't it be great if that relationship looked different!* **We've seen many relationships totally transform because somebody believed that something different *could* be possible—and then took action to make it a reality.** Despite the limiting beliefs running through your head, you have the power to make this change happen.

Ask yourself, *What would I love my relationships to look like one year from today?* Whatever relationship you want to improve, this could be the year.

RELATIONSHIP EXAMPLES

- I feel proud of where I am in my life. I'm being kind to myself and giving myself the benefit of the doubt.
- I have a productive working relationship with my manager. I feel appreciated, and I'm getting valuable coaching.
- My parents and I are close. We talk often, and even though we live a couple hours apart, I see them monthly, which brings me a lot of joy.
- I am in a meaningful romantic relationship that gives me the love and companionship I want in life. My partner and I spend time together doing things we both love to do, and we pursue our own interests, too.

PUTTING IT ALL TOGETHER

Your vision should be authentically yours. It should be inspiring and a usable tool. Whether you're reading it or sharing it with other people (a critical step that we'll get to in the next chapter), it will have a greater impact if it's more than a bulleted list of statements. We recommend weaving your responses to the questions into a full vision that resonates with you and that paints a full picture of where you'll be one year from today.

So where do you start? Some people lead with their outlook or what they want to be known for. From there, you can organize it based on what's most important to you, pulling together elements from your answers. For instance, you might have a section on your marriage where you address a way that you want to grow personally (maybe doing a better job of devoting time to the important people in your life) as well as your vision for how that relationship will look in one year.

Also consider including your answer to the question "What would be possible if you let this belief go?" from the limiting beliefs exercise. As you write, mention the things you are grateful for, proud of, or that are working in your life now so that you don't lose sight of them.

In the end, how you pull your vision together is up to you. We've included examples in our workbook, available at FastForwardGroup.net/Book to inspire you. Whatever you choose and however you create it, make sure it's something you can easily access and refer back to frequently.

You have one life. It is your job to find a way to be lit up in it. Nobody is going to do it for you. The circumstances of your life will probably not change unless you decide to change them. Writing a bold vision is your best bet for creating the kind of clarity and creative energy that will help you generate peace, happiness, and success. It's the most effective way of empowering yourself, of becoming intentional with your choices, of crafting a life that makes you feel proud and fulfilled.

The good news is that you don't have to go it alone. In the next chapter, we'll show you how to start building the support you need to turn your vision into reality.

Chapter 4

IMPROVE YOUR ODDS: ENROLL PEOPLE IN YOUR VISION

B y the time Georgia left the large company where she'd worked for more than a decade, she had a lot of "relational capital." She knew people at the top of the organization well, and they knew her. She was respected and extremely well-liked. She knew how to get things done. She probably couldn't pick up the phone and call the CEO, but if she wanted to talk with the national head of her division, she could.

At her new company, she knew almost nobody. This was a problem, because she had a vision for her career that required the company to do something dramatic: to partner with a *competing* industry. She knew the idea would churn up some internal resistance, *and* she wanted to lead the effort as head of a newly formed department. Before even applying for the job, she had talked with friends at the company, had done deep research into its performance and challenges, and had done the same with the competing industry and the major players who might make good partners. She knew it could work. First, she had to get people *who didn't know her well* to buy into her vision.

Every new person in her department met with Todd, the president of the division, and Georgia's meeting was coming up fast. She had about thirty minutes to make an impression that could have a profound impact on her year and career. How could she let him know who she was, how passionate she was about her work, *and* get him thinking about a different possible future?

On the day of the meeting, she walked into his office and, after some quick pleasantries, said, "I'd like to start by sharing my vision with you so you can see how I see my future here. I'd love your feedback." She proceeded to read her entire vision to him—her professional and her personal goals. As he listened, his eyes grew wide. When she was done, he thanked her for her vulnerability and for the insights she had shared about herself and the company. He told her that nobody had ever been this transparent in his new employee meetings, and that he appreciated it.

Georgia had participated in our Fast Forward program a few years before moving companies and had used her first bold vision to change departments, something that wasn't easy to do. She had used her vision every year since to advance her career and accomplish important personal goals. Even for a "vision veteran" like Georgia, it required a lot of vulnerability and courage to share her vision with this leader the first time she met him.

Two months after her meeting, Todd called her and said, "I'd like you to start laying the groundwork for the new partnership department. What would it look like? How would we go about approaching leaders in the industry and building trust?" One year later, she was leading a team focused on partnerships and crushing it.

Georgia had enrolled people in her vision. She had painted a vivid picture of what she saw for the future. In sharing it, she helped others see that future, too. They could get excited about it, which encouraged them to support it. Think back to Kennedy's Man on the Moon speech. Sharing that vision so clearly and vividly motivated people to get on board. The goal would have been impossible without the support and creativity of many, many people.

Too many visions stay tucked away in a journal or hidden in our heads as vague concepts. When we don't tell people what we're going for, our chances of accomplishing it become pretty slim. It's like we can see what's on the other side of the wall, but we're refusing to throw our hats over it. Remember, the action word in this Power Principle is "declare"—*declare* a bold vision, not imagine it or think about it or create it or dream it up.

**Declaring is where a lot of your power
to create change comes from.**

If you want to turn your hope for a year of extraordinary success into *actual* extraordinary success, you have to build your commitment, motivation, and accountability. You can't do that without support, which requires sharing your vision. In this chapter, we'll cover the essentials of sharing your vision in a way that builds excitement and progress. We'll address the mental roadblocks that might come up and how to overcome them. We'll also get practical and offer a helpful guide for sharing it with people. We'll help you identify a person who could become your "vision buddy" for support and accountability.

You can't do anything bold alone, so enrolling other people in your vision is the best way to improve your odds of success.

SAYING IS BELIEVING, AND OTHER REASONS TO SHARE

Psychology professor Gail Matthews decided it was time to test some of the frequently repeated goal-achievement truisms. She found that yes, writing your goals down dramatically improves your odds of achieving them—it makes them 42 percent more likely to happen![1] This is one reason we structure our vision exercise the way we do. But *telling* somebody about your goals—especially if it's somebody whose opinion matters to you—and asking them to hold you accountable makes accomplishing them even more likely. People in Matthews's study who told a friend and then sent them regular progress reports scored their progress and accomplishments 25 percent higher than those who only wrote their goals down.

One reason this works is because of what psychologists call the "saying is believing" effect. **When we say things out loud to other people, especially when our goal is to create a "shared reality," it shifts our own perception of the things we say.[2] We believe them more.** Our participants experience this too—they've repeatedly told us that when they share their visions, the goals and outcomes become more "real." (Note that in the next chapter, we'll explain how this can be both a benefit and a drawback.) As one person said, "It seemed like the more I shared about what I wanted and what I was doing, the more it propelled me to do what came next." Yes, that's exactly what happens.

As we worked with more and more people over the years, we also learned that, when we share our visions, the people we share with often relate to our goals as a foregone conclusion. They nod their heads and say, "Right. Of course. That makes total sense." **They have faith that we'll make it happen—often more faith than we do—and that helps us overcome limiting beliefs and feel more confident.**

Sharing also gives us access to ideas and information we need to achieve our goals. One of our cognitive biases is to assume that other people know what we know, not that they might know something we don't. Even when we're going for something we aren't sure how to achieve, we often don't think to ask other people for advice. When we share our visions, though, people get enthused and start sharing strategies they've used to achieve similar things. Sometimes we learn the one thing that can make the biggest difference.

Psychologists and sociologists have written much about the power of our social networks to influence our behavior and our ability to achieve goals. As human beings, we learn by observing, without even realizing it. If we're intentional about it, we can use that innate habit to our advantage. In *How to Change*, Katy Milkman describes a strategy she calls "copy and paste." "When we're unsure of ourselves," Milkman writes, "a powerful way the people around us can help boost our capacity and confidence is by showing us what's possible."[3] Even if they aren't intentionally offering advice, they're educating and informing our decisions just by letting us watch them work. The more we share our vision, the more likely it is that we'll be connected to groups or networks of people who are doing the very thing we're trying to do, so that we can copy and paste more.

When we ask people who have shared their visions how it felt and what happened next, their stories are incredible. Recall Jonah from chapter two, who shared his vision to leave sales and work in training and development with his boss. He was surprised by how supportive she was. She introduced him and his work to people in HR and learning and development. She connected him to leaders in other departments who were struggling with training their teams, so that he could build a case for more internal training. She connected him with people who had shifted careers within the company, so that he could understand what roadblocks he might face. She gave him even more opportunities to do training work with the team so that he could keep learning. Because of her support, his vision became possible.

THE TRUTH: SHARING MAKES US UNCOMFORTABLE

Even though you know Georgia's story turned out well, can you imagine doing what she did? Did it make you cringe to picture her sitting in an office with somebody she didn't know and being that open and vulnerable? That's how most of us feel when we think about talking about our big dreams—exposed or naked. We hold back, and then we miss the opportunity!

In our programs, everyone gets a Fast Forward "buddy" who can be a peer coach, sounding board, and accountability partner (more on this in a bit). One of our participants was paired with somebody he thought he knew well. After they met and shared their visions with each other, he told us, "I've known this person for a decade, and I learned more about him in those five minutes than I had in the previous ten years." That's inspiring, but also a little alarming. Why had this colleague never shared his whole, real, authentic self as he did that day?

As we've said, when we declare our visions, we're putting ourselves on the hook for making them happen, and that creates fear. We're afraid to be held accountable, especially for bold visions that we aren't sure how to accomplish. What if we tell our boss we want to go for something and we don't make it? What will they think about our abilities the next time an opportunity opens up?

Beyond fear of failing, though, **we're afraid of being vulnerable. We're afraid of people's judgment, and we're even more afraid of their cynicism or skepticism.** (Remember Lisa's husband's response—"We'll see"—when she told him she wanted to be known for being calm and present.) If people doubt us or our goals, or even the fundamental idea that change is possible, it might dim our enthusiasm and lessen our courage. We know that naysayers can suck the energy out of us. And what might we learn about other people and what they think of us that we didn't necessarily want to?

Our discomfort with vulnerability also supports the habit of compartmentalizing ourselves. We present a "work self" at work and our "true self" or "other self" in our personal lives. Sharing your vision breaks that cycle and offers you an opportunity to bring your "whole self" to all aspects of your life, which leads to more authentic, meaningful, open relationships. Being more authentic at work (something that is difficult for close to 30 percent of people) boosts your job satisfaction and your performance.[4]

Sometimes our hesitation is about time. Given the demands of work, we think we don't have time to get to know people or don't want to take up their time talking about ourselves. If you think you need a bunch of happy hours or lunches to connect with your colleagues or build a more cohesive team, try spending a few minutes reading your visions to each other. It's an effective and efficient way to relate deeply with them. Outside of work, sharing deepens our relationships or helps us make tough decisions about key relationships.

>>

Sharing your vision requires you to be vulnerable, profoundly changing your relationship with the listener.

>>

As we've said, people are usually surprised by how much support they get when they share their goals and dreams. **But even people who encountered skepticism rather than unbridled enthusiasm found that sharing was helpful.** For some, it compelled them to prove people wrong. For some, it opened up a valuable conversation that provided even more clarity and support in the long-term. And for some, it spurred them to make a big decision.

That's what happened for Mita Mallick, host of the Brown Table Talk podcast and head of diversity, equity, and inclusion for Carta. She had grown up painfully shy and had been raised to be quietly ambitious. The idea of sharing her vision was difficult because she had never advocated for the things she wanted or for her own success. A year or two after writing her first vision, she felt ready for the next big career move. She heard about a role that was opening up in her company that would give her an opportunity to do more of the work she had outlined in her vision. Another leader in the company had told her it would be a great job for her. She met with her manager to express her interest. "I heard this position is opening up," she said, "and I'd love to put my name on the slate to be considered."

He looked at her and said, "You have two young children at home. There's no way you can travel that much. You can't do that job. No."

She was so stunned by the response that she didn't say much before leaving. When she thought about it later, she realized she shouldn't have been surprised. Her manager had made similar, if less overt, comments in the past about her ability to grow her career and be a working parent. He would never be an avid supporter of her vision for her career. She had to accept that, but she didn't have to let it stop her. She simply looked for support elsewhere, finding it from peers and leaders within her organization and from others in her network as she shared her aspirations. She continued to do great work in her role, to volunteer for big projects that gave her exposure to other leaders, and to find opportunities to build skills she knew she was lacking. And within eighteen months, she was recommended for a position with another company for an even better role.

This is what most of us fear will happen when we share our vision—that we'll be shot down—but it's rare. And when it does happen, it presents an opportunity to reassess and find your true supporters.

When people come up to Wendy in a workshop and push back on sharing their vision, she always says, "Tell me more. What's making you uncomfortable?" The more you can understand the limiting beliefs holding you back from sharing your vision, the easier it will be to overcome them. Are there specific pieces of your vision that you're especially worried about sharing? Why? Are there specific people you feel uncomfortable sharing it with? Why? What's the worst that could happen? And the most important question: **What would be possible if you *enrolled* people in your vision?**

No one that we've met has ever regretted sharing their vision. Most say that once they did, a whole world of support, connection, and possibility opened up for them—or at the very least, they gained a lot of clarity.

WHO TO SHARE WITH, AND HOW

Choosing who to share your vision with is simple. Just ask yourself, "Who can help me make this happen?" Usually, that means a handful of people, including a manager, a mentor, our colleagues, the people on the team we lead, our spouses or partners, and important family members and friends. The more people you tell, the more help you'll get.

Does anything about that list make you uncomfortable right off the bat? If so, ask why and then see if you can make it more comfortable by choosing parts of your vision to share. If your vision includes moving to a new position and that means leaving your team, it may not be appropriate to share that with them. If your vision involves spicing up your sex life with your spouse, it's probably not appropriate to share that with colleagues or your parents or kids. (But your friends might be able to offer some strategies! You know who they are.)

Share as much as you possibly can with the people who can offer the most support.

Overcoming the discomfort of who to share with is the first step. The next step is getting past the discomfort of how. One challenge of sharing our vision with people is that we're obviously doing it because we want their support. It feels like we're making a request—because we are—and as we'll explore in Power Principle 4, we are *really* uncomfortable with making requests. Again, this is where our power to shape our lives comes from. **If we can't ask for what we want or need to achieve our goals, how can we expect to get it?**

Because we're so uncomfortable, we get nervous, make common missteps, and then aren't happy with the response we get. We blindside people with the conversation, springing it on them when they're not ready to focus on what we're saying. We use disclaimers like "This may sound crazy" or "I know this seems unrealistic" to avoid taking a stand or making too big of a commitment. We also rush through the telling, talking fast or skimming over pieces that feel especially bold. And we go into these discussions without a clear idea of the kind of support we're looking for. We aren't specific about what we need, and then we're disappointed when we don't get it.

To help you overcome these tendencies, here's a simple approach to the conversation that you can use with almost anybody.

VISION SHARING GUIDE

1. **Clear distractions.** Set a time to talk and make sure it's free of distractions. The person should be able to focus on what you're sharing.

2. **Give them context.** Say something like, "Recently, I decided to be more intentional about where my life was heading, so I wrote a vision of what success could look like one year from today. It covers all the things that I want personally and professionally. I'd like to share it with you because I'd like your feedback and support." You could use this language when asking for a meeting or a dinner to set expectations.

3. **Read it out loud.** Once they're on board, read your vision to them **slowly and clearly**, omitting anything you're not comfortable sharing. Remember, **skip the disclaimers!** They diminish your impact. After you meet, you could also share the written version with them so they aren't expected to remember the details from one conversation.

4. **Request what you need.**
   o If you're talking with your boss, you might ask for feedback to ensure you're aligned on important priorities related to your job and your development. Or you might ask for their support or resources.
   o If you are sharing with a spouse, partner, or friend, you might ask for them to hold you accountable or to support you in other ways. For instance, if you need to block time for something specific outside of work, you might ask your partner to take on some of your usual household responsibilities. If you're

intending to be healthier, you might ask a friend to change your usual Friday happy hour to a walk. Whatever it is you need, be specific in the request, offer ideas for what it could look like, and listen with an open mind to the other person's ideas.

FIND A BUDDY

When it comes to our own success or well-being, we're not great at holding ourselves accountable. It's easy to let our priorities be consumed by other people's wants and needs and the day-to-day fire alarms of life. That's why we recommend that you share your vision in the first place. We also encourage you to take it one step further and find a "vision buddy" who you can talk to about your whole vision and who can serve as a sounding board and an accountability partner. Remember the data: If you ask somebody to hold you accountable, you'll be much more likely to accomplish your goals.

Your buddy is there to help you do what you say you will do and be who you say you will be.

When you're thinking about candidates, you want somebody who will be a positive, supportive force, but who won't let you off the hook. They'll be willing to challenge you if your limiting beliefs or old habits are getting in the way of what you want, or if they think you're not prioritizing it. Ideally, this person is somebody who can be objective about your life, which means it probably isn't anybody named in your vision. When we assign Fast Forward Buddies in our programs, for example, we don't pair people with their managers.

If you ask somebody to be your buddy, let them know that you're willing to play the same role for them, in whatever way they need. Hearing you talk about your vision could inspire them to throw *their* hat over the wall.

We feel certain that someone, probably many people, in your life are willing to help you succeed. You just need to ask. Once you do, plan to meet with your buddy once a month to discuss your progress, successes, struggles, or decisions.

TIPS FOR USING YOUR VISION

The rest of this book is designed to help you achieve your vision. The Power Principles will help you shift your perspective about assumed hurdles and obstacles, turn your vision into a manageable 90-day action plan, and improve your communication skills so that you can make more things happen with other people. Your vision will be your north star as you work through the rest of the Power Principles and the exercises we'll share. That said, it's okay to keep reading and come back to writing your vision later. You might learn things that influence what you include.

Before we move on, we want to share some helpful tips for using your vision to provide inspiration and focus throughout the year. **It should be more than a hope or a dream—it should be a tool.**

Make Your Vision Accessible and Visible
- Make it available on your laptop, phone, and tablet, or anywhere else that gives you quick and easy access, no matter where you are or when you might need to look at it.
- Print it out and keep a hard copy somewhere you will see it often.
- Share it (or parts of it) digitally with people you've asked for support.

Track Your Progress

- Put a recurring fifteen-minute monthly appointment on your calendar and spend the time rereading your vision to reorient yourself to your north star.
- Track your progress toward your goals quarterly, ideally with an accountability partner or buddy. Make adjustments based on how far you've come or what you've learned.

Review, and Then Do It All Again

- At the end of the year, review your progress, assess gaps, and take time to celebrate and feel proud of how far you've come. Most people do not accomplish 100 percent of their bold vision because they're playing big. But as we've said, they still accomplish much more than they would have if they hadn't gone for what they really wanted.
- Then it's time to throw your hat over the wall again for the coming year with an updated bold vision. Some elements stay on your vision year after year because they are still important and still unpredictable, like Lisa's effort to be calm and present. Some elements become too predictable and aren't necessary any longer.

If you're ready to throw your hat over the wall, to declare your bold vision and commit to making it happen, take ten minutes and read your vision to somebody (or multiple people). They'll learn the most important things about you—how you define extraordinary success for the future and your ambitions and dreams for your whole life. You will be amazed by how many people want to help—and what a difference that makes!

Now it's time to start getting rid of obstacles and taking action to make the life you want a reality.

CHOOSE A NEW PERSPECTIVE

What's the Cost of Being Right?

Chapter 5

STORIES YOUR BRAIN MAKES UP—AND WHAT THEY COST YOU

You are a half-hour into your day when your phone chimes with a text from your boss: "Please call me asap."

What's the first thought that comes to mind? It's probably not, *I've been nominated for an award* or *She loved the report I sent*. Suddenly, your mood has plummeted, your palms are sweaty, and you want to do just about anything other than make that call.

Then, two minutes later, you get another text: "I've got an idea for today's meeting that I want to run by you."

We've all starred in this movie at some point—because we're human. In the last thirty days, you probably created a mental story in response to something that happened. Maybe it was a confusing email from your biggest client or a non-response from the person you've been dating for six months. You spent time and emotional energy worrying about it, creating stress and anxiety in your day. And then it turned out to be fine, or better than fine. You were relieved, but you also felt emotionally or mentally exhausted.

Even though *most* of what happens to *most* of us in any given day is neutral or positive, our assumptions or predictions tend to be negative. (Remember our discussion of cognitive bias in chapter two.) We add significance and drama to situations and circumstances, often when there's no proof of either. In the early years of building our business, Lisa used to get anxious when she didn't hear back from a potential client within a week, saying to herself and others, "I came on too strong" and "I've wasted time on that proposal." Then she'd get a response, and everything would be fine. We all do this, especially in our always-on, hyper-connected world. In his book *Soundtracks*, Jon Acuff wrote, "I've listened to 'Sweet Child O' Mine' a thousand times. I've listened to 'That friend didn't respond to your text message because they're mad' a *hundred thousand* times."[1]

If you're telling yourself positive stories, like "I did so well in that presentation" or "I've never looked better," great! Keep going. What we want to help you tackle are the negative, disempowering stories that create unnecessary suffering, stress, and anxiety.

Some stories can be short-lived, like the examples above, but the more costly stories are those that we have been telling ourselves and reinforcing for months, years, even decades—like "My boss doesn't appreciate me," "That team doesn't care," or "Nothing I do is good enough for my parents." These stories convince us that some things simply cannot be changed, cannot be any better than they are right now. They have a big impact on our happiness, confidence, resilience, relationships, and well-being.

For all these reasons, **our disempowering stories keep us from creating the life we want and keep us from achieving our visions.** They're often interwoven with our limiting beliefs. They influence how we behave in the present, so they influence what's possible in the future. They self-perpetuate.

In the next two chapters, we'll show you that it doesn't have to be this way. You don't have to let these stories continue to play out. You can change the narrative.

>>

You have zero control over other people and many circumstances, but you have 100 percent choice in your perspective.

>>

We've known this for thousands of years. The Stoic philosopher-king Marcus Aurelius, writing about how to respond to the things that happen to us, said, "*Choose* not to be harmed—and you won't feel harmed. Don't feel harmed—and you haven't been . . . It doesn't hurt me unless I interpret its happening as harmful to me. I can choose not to."[2]

When you choose a more empowering perspective, the ripple effects of positive change can be profound. It helps to start by understanding the source of your stories and their impact in your life. As you may have noticed in the last two sentences, we use the words "story" and "perspective" interchangeably.

In this chapter, we'll explain how your brain creates narratives and then works to prove them by collecting evidence that they're true, that you're "right." We'll explore the common costs of this, and especially how you might be creating self-fulfilling prophecies. Finally, we'll give you a simple exercise for recognizing and identifying your disempowering stories and acknowledging what they're costing you. Recognizing the cost of your mindset and behavior is the first step to changing them so that you can create the life you want.

FACTS VERSUS STORIES

Wendy: My son, Ben, was "challenging" from an early age. In kindergarten, he couldn't sit still during circle time, so had to sit in the teacher's lap. In first grade, he was always getting in trouble. He would sometimes hurt the kids he was playing with—not intentionally, but because he was a bit wild. He broke one kid's finger and hit another in the eye with a block. At home, he seemed to constantly irritate his sisters—more so than other younger brothers I knew.

Because of this, I would say to myself and other people on a regular basis, "I love him, but he is a pain in the ass." Every morning I would wake up and there would be more evidence that this was true. One of the girls would be crying or I'd get another call from the school or I'd trip over his stuff because it was scattered everywhere.

That was the story I told about my son. And as long as I kept telling it and kept believing that it was the truth, that's who he was—which is heartbreaking for me even now, ten years later.

With all of his energy, it's not surprising that Ben loved sports. He was on a Little League team and had an excellent coach. At the end of the season the coach called me to talk about Ben. *Oh no*, I thought, *here it comes*, braced for more proof that I was *right* about Ben. But this is what he said: "Ben is a really inspiring kid. When he gets up to bat, unlike a lot of kids his age, he has guts and tenacity. He gets this look of determination and a big smile and then takes a huge swing. His courage is inspiring. I've loved working with him this season."

I thanked him and hung up the phone. This person who had only known Ben for a few months had a completely different story from mine about who he was and what he had to offer. And it was just as true as my story. I realized right then that I had to stop telling my story about Ben. Instead, I chose the coach's story. Since that day, what I say about my son to myself and others is, "Ben is courageous and inspiring." And I look for evidence to support that every day.

The brain is a meaning-making machine. It collects bits of information and uses them to interpret the world—to create a story. Wendy's brain combined what she learned about Ben with her other life experiences and pulled it all together (with a slant toward the negative) to create a story about who Ben was and what she should expect of him. As we wrote in chapter two, the brain does this so that it can quickly interpret what's happening now and predict what will happen next—to keep us alive.

Our stories become the lens through which we see the world. They influence how we perceive people and situations and what we expect about our future. Here's the problem: They are based on our *perception* and the brain's *interpretation*. They are *not* reality or fact.

Facts are indisputable data points, without much emotion or drama. Your perspective is a story your brain makes up about those facts. "I'm in a meeting speaking to eight people" is a fact. "I'm doing a great job of sharing my ideas with my team" is a story or perspective (a good one!). "I am forty-eight" is a fact. "I'm getting old" is a perspective. "He's been my manager for three years" is a fact. "He's never going to put me up for promotion" is a perspective.

Facts	Story
• 0% control	• 100% choice
• Fixed, indisputable	• We believe it's the objective truth
• No drama	• We collect evidence
	• It has a *cost* if it's negative

We relate to our perspective like it's the *only* perspective, like it's the *truth* — but it usually is not.

If something is the *truth*, there can't be any other possibilities, which means the story can't change, and the future can't look different than the past. We'll be stuck in that story until we *choose* to change it. While we may not be able to control the facts, we *can* control the story we tell ourselves and other people. When we do, it's like we've chosen to put on a different pair of glasses. We see the world differently.

First, we have to raise our consciousness of where our brains are working hardest to prove that we're right about our stories.

Collecting Evidence and Cementing Your Stories

One of the most challenging biases afflicting all of us is confirmation bias. For decades, study after study has shown that we look for, prioritize, trust, and remember information that supports what we already believe to be true. (The concept was first studied by psychologist Peter Wason in 1960,[3] though the phrase was not introduced until 1977.[4]) We *interpret* situations and interactions in ways that confirm our perspectives.

Every day, we collect evidence that confirms our stories.

We find that evidence everywhere, even within our own words. In the last chapter, we described the "saying is believing" effect. The more we say things out loud, the more we believe them. This can work for us or against us. Every time Wendy told her story about Ben to somebody else, her brain interpreted it as proof.

We don't have room to cover *all* the cognitive biases that help cement our stories, especially our negative stories. What's important to know is that the more your brain collects evidence for the thing you believe is true, the truer it feels, and the easier it becomes to find evidence to support it, and so on. You will continue to believe that story, sometimes even when you're given evidence it's not true.

The day after the space shuttle *Challenger* exploded, two researchers asked college students where they were, what they were doing, and who they were with when they heard the news. Just three years later, the researchers asked the same questions of the same students—and 40 percent of them gave different answers. When the researchers showed the students their original answers, many assumed the first answers were wrong or even that they had lied.[5] They had developed stories that changed their memories of the facts—and they believed those stories absolutely.

Over time, it becomes harder to challenge your stories—but that doesn't mean you can't! It takes mental and sometimes emotional effort and fortitude. But the cost of not making the effort is high.

THE COST OF BEING "RIGHT"

Somewhere in your life, you're probably collecting evidence for a disempowering story. Despite all the proof and despite how true and right it feels (my manager really *doesn't* appreciate me, that client really *is* an egotistical jerk, my mother-in-law really *is* hypercritical of my parenting), it's still just a story. And the person suffering in that story is you.

Your negative stories cost you happiness, productivity, relationships, connection, and well-being. That's a high cost—which is why it's important to challenge them and ultimately to choose an empowering story instead.

———————————— >> ————————————

You can choose to be right, or you can choose to be happy.

———————————— >> ————————————

Your willingness to give up a negative story begins when you recognize what the story is costing you.

> **Lisa:** Years ago, I joined a new company to lead their sales organization. My first step as a new leader was to meet with each of my direct reports one-on-one. In these meetings, as I asked questions about strengths, challenges, and opportunities, a common "story" quickly emerged about the research team: "They're incompetent." "They don't understand the pressure we're under to hit goals." "They're so slow." To the sales team, these were

longstanding "truths." They had been collecting evidence for the story for years.

I knew the research team was key to our success, so I set out to learn more. When I interviewed the research leaders, I heard an equally toxic story: "The sales team treats us like doormats." "They set unrealistic deadlines; they don't appreciate the effort and time involved in our work." "We send them information and then never hear back. Our work goes into a black hole and we don't know if it was useful or pointless."

Clearly these respective stories had a high cost to our business and culture. I had no control over their story, but I could influence my team's story. So that's what I set out to do.

In our next meeting, I shared what I learned and my concerns about the situation given our ambitious goals.

Then I asked, "What is the cost to us of this negative perspective about them?" It wasn't hard to get answers, because they were all paying the price: limited collaboration, frustration, anger, stress about deadlines and hitting sales targets, and resignation that it wouldn't improve. Because they perceived the story as "the truth," they spent a lot of time complaining about the problems rather than trying to solve them.

Recognizing the costs in this way flipped a switch for the team. It helped them see how much they were suffering—needlessly. We decided that from then on, our perspective on the research team would be that they were essential to our success and that we were one team. We didn't believe it—yet—but given the costs, we were willing to practice it. Looking through that new lens, we took some actions and changed how we interacted with them. We stopped complaining about them. We invited two research leaders to attend our weekly meeting so they could hear the sales challenges we were facing firsthand. We became more conscious of our timelines and the number of requests we were submitting, making sure they were valid and necessary. We acknowledged their work on a regular basis and made them feel part of solutions and growth. Over time, the new story that we chose was game-changing for our business.

Can you relate to this situation, professionally or personally? Think of the last time you got together with family and spent time rehashing a common story about somebody else in the family, based on fresh evidence. **The only thing more costly than a disempowering individual story is a disempowering group story.** Our cognitive biases are compounded when we tell a story as a group, proving to ourselves and each other how right we all are every time we tell it.[6]

Regardless of how your story might be playing out right now, you can choose to change it at any time.

THE GOOD NEWS: YOU AREN'T STUCK WITH YOUR STORIES

Along with her colleagues, well-known psychologist and mindset researcher Carol Dweck taught a group of low-performing seventh graders about the "malleability of intelligence"—that we can grow our intelligence by thinking of the brain like a muscle. As she recounted, "All at once Jimmy—the most hard-core turned-off low-effort kid in the group—looked up with tears in his eyes and said, 'You mean, I don't have to be dumb?' From that day on, he worked. He started staying up late to do his homework, which he never used to bother with at all. He started handing in assignments early so he could get feedback and revise them."[7] Jimmy became convinced of a different story, and it made all the difference.

Choosing a new perspective, or telling yourself a different story, is like staging an intervention in your own life. You choose a different path, and your experience is never the same again.

You might be thinking, "Saying something doesn't make it true." If so, you may be missing two points. First, your current perspective often isn't any truer than another perspective, so why *not* choose a more positive and empowering one? Second, saying something *can* change how you feel and what you perceive to be possible. Remember, language creates reality. Once we can see and describe a different future, it changes how we act and how we treat people.

Let's go back to Wendy and Ben to see how.

Wendy: Soon after my revelation about Ben, a big group of us went to Disneyland. It was crowded and hot, and after spending the morning running around, we were tired and hungry. We picked a spot for lunch and grabbed a table big enough for all of us. The lines to order food were long and all we wanted to do was sit.

We were debating who was going to make the sacrifice and get in line when little Ben piped up. Keep in mind that at the time, he was seven or eight years old. "I'll do it!" he said. I'm sure we all looked a bit skeptical, because he insisted: "I can do it! Just tell me what you want." It tells you something about how desperate and exhausted we were that we handed him a wad of money and sent him off with the order.

Ben got in line, waited patiently, placed the whole order by himself, paid, waited for them to fill the order, then ran back and forth to get the food to the table. When somebody realized their order was wrong, he took it back, went straight to the front of the line despite a lot of grumbling from the waiting adults, showed the cashier the receipt, and got the correct meal.

How many kids his age could have done that?

If I had held onto my original story about Ben that day, I might have focused on how hard it was to keep track of him in the crowds or how often he bumped into other people in line or how many times one of his sisters complained about something he did. But because I had chosen a different story, this is what I remember about that day. Those other things probably happened, given what I know about Ben at that age—but I don't remember them.

I was collecting evidence for a different story, and I found it on a regular basis. This made my story more "the truth" for me, and consequently for Ben and for all the people in my life who know him. Today, as a teenager, he's one of the most independent and capable people I know. We are incredibly close, even now in his teenage years, because we have *mutual* admiration, love, and respect for each other, which began with me taking on a new perspective about him.

How to Spot and Begin to Change a Disempowering Story

In this chapter and the next, we're going to share our model for choosing to pursue a dramatically different perspective on all kinds of situations, experiences, and relationships. It is based on psychological strategies for *cognitive reappraisal*, which is just a ten-dollar phrase for changing your perspective on situations where you might be suffering.

In a nutshell, here's the process.

1. Identify your disempowering perspective.
2. Identify the facts.
3. Identify the costs.
4. Brainstorm new possible perspectives, and choose the one that resonates with you most.
5. Identify what will be different in how you think, speak, and act as a result of your new perspective.

Let's break this down. Before you can change any disempowering stories you tell yourself, you have to identify them and become more conscious of their impact, day to day. That's what we're tackling in this chapter. Start by considering these questions.

- Is there a situation or relationship in your life that's causing you stress, limiting your happiness, or sapping your energy?

- Is there a problem in your life that has been with you for a long time and that you haven't been able to solve or overcome?
- Is there something you regularly complain about, but don't take action to change?
- Is there a worry that comes up often, that is keeping you awake at night, that is looming in your life and overshadowing your joy?

If you're a human being, the answer to at least one of these questions is probably yes, and behind that answer is likely a disempowering story. Here's a list of some common ones that you might relate to. Because they are similar concepts, you might see the similarities between this list and the limiting beliefs examples.

Personal Examples	Professional Examples
• They don't appreciate me. • My mother is so critical—nothing is ever good enough. • It's hard to meet someone. • I'm not a good parent. • It's hard to be healthy. • There aren't enough hours in the day. • My partner does nothing around the house; I have to do everything.	• I'm overwhelmed and constantly behind. • I should be further along in my career. • My manager doesn't care about my growth. • My clients don't respect me or value my contributions. • It's hard to find work-life balance in this company. • That team is incompetent.

Use what you discover here to tackle the first three steps in the process of change.

EXERCISE: UNDERSTANDING YOUR DISEMPOWERING PERSPECTIVES

1. What is one of your disempowering perspectives?
   - Choose one with some heat, one that brings up feelings of stress, angst, or anger, or that you think will keep you from achieving your vision.
2. What are the facts?
   - Push yourself to list only absolute, objective, undeniable facts, not interpretations. Be careful not to rely on your memories.
3. What is it costing you?
   - Consider the obvious and less obvious or far-reaching costs to you and to others.

Your negative stories can and will impede progress toward your vision. They can get in the way of your goals, your confidence, and your happiness. Now here's the good news: you have 100 percent control over them, even if it doesn't feel that way. In the next chapter, we're going to show you how to take back the narratives defining your life.

Chapter 6

IT'S YOUR STORY.
YOU GET TO CHOOSE IT.

When Emma was presented with her new job opportunity, her stomach sank. It was a promotion, but it wasn't a role she wanted. It meant moving into a department that she knew little about, and one that was struggling. The leadership team was clear that they needed a strong leader to turn it around. She felt her only choice was to say yes—a "step up or step out" situation.

When we began working with her soon after her role change, we saw that negative, disempowering story reflected in everything she said, things like "This is never going to work" and "It's just the worst." This story was especially detrimental *because* the team wasn't performing up to expectations and had recently lost some talent. It was Emma's responsibility to recruit new people. She started by reaching out to people she believed would be a good fit, but early on in each conversation, her negativity would creep in. When you lead with "This is so broken . . . will you help me fix it?" convincing somebody to come onboard is a hard sell.

When we shared the concept of choosing a new perspective, she immediately saw the high cost of the story she was telling herself. As long as her perspective was so negative, she could not be happy in the role and wouldn't be successful as a leader. She wasn't being fair to her new team or herself, so she started with the facts: First, they had *asked* her to take the role. When they did, they had told her they had faith in her ability to make a positive impact. The next fact was that she had said yes. She could have said no and sought a role at another company, but she hadn't. Now she had a choice. She could choose to be "right" about how terrible the situation was, or she could choose to be happy.

She put the negative story and all the evidence she had collected to one side and reframed the situation, trying to find a new lens. The new position was more visible because it was a turnaround situation. The whole leadership team was looking to her to improve the department's operations, culture, and results. If she could make it work, it could accelerate her career. It was also a massive learning opportunity, with exposure to an aspect of the business she didn't know much about. She saw potential in the team, and she had leeway to hire the people she thought she needed.

It took a bit of work, but Emma was able to choose a new, empowering perspective. She not only stayed in the role, she thrived in it. She showcased talents she didn't even realize she had and focused on the kind of work she loved doing. She built a strong team and developed better processes for the department. A couple of years later, she was promoted again into a new position that she still loves. Recently, she said, "You can pitch any situation twenty-five different ways, and how you pitch it influences how you internalize it, how you react to it, and how everyone else perceives you in it."

Doing what Emma did takes discipline and practice. When we aren't happy or fulfilled, it's easy to keep looking for evidence of the old, disempowering story and to keep being "right." Sometimes, we focus on a specific action we could take to change the situation but that doesn't change the underlying issue (think about people you know who have moved to a new city or to a new company, but still aren't happy). Even if we *do* shift our perspective, we often don't go far enough or we focus on a point in the future when things will be different. For instance, imagine if Emma's perspective was, "Okay, I'm stuck here, but I just have to make it work for two years and then I can reasonably ask to be moved." Would she have been successful in the role? Probably not. And she definitely would not have been happy. To fundamentally change our experience, we need to fundamentally change our perspective.

Choosing a new perspective is one of the most empowering steps you can take to improve your life in the present and in the future.

In this chapter, we're going to continue guiding you through our five-step process for choosing a new perspective. First, we'll help you reframe your negative story by brainstorming more positive stories to tell yourself instead. Then we'll explore how to put the new perspective into practice. As you do this, you'll begin to see things differently, believe in new possibilities, and get unstuck from your perception of "the truth." You'll begin behaving differently, more in line with the life you want now and in the future. Giving yourself a new pair of glasses for viewing circumstances and relationships *is* possible—and it *will* make your vision more possible, too.

HOW TO CHOOSE AN EMPOWERING PERSPECTIVE

Abigail, a client of ours, has one sibling, Leanne, who is three years younger than she is. They're both married and have children who are about the same age. Abigail lives in Texas, and Leanne lives in a suburb of New York City. Abigail had a negative story about Leanne, which she shared with us during a session: "My sister and I aren't close. We're too different. She doesn't really care about what's going on in my life. She's jealous of my success." Abigail was resigned to this being "the truth."

The costs of her story were high. It made Abigail sad. She felt she was missing an important relationship in her life, especially when her friends would talk about their close ties with brothers and sisters. *She* felt jealous when she heard about Leanne going on vacations with her brother-in-law. Family gatherings could be tense because people would get pulled into taking sides. Abigail also felt like her kids were missing out on a close relationship with their cousins. While examining her story and the fallout in a Fast Forward program, she had a moment of clarity. She didn't want it to be this way anymore, and she knew if she didn't do anything about it, nothing would change.

What could Abigail do? Trying to change her sister was a terrible idea (trying to change *anybody* is a terrible idea). She also couldn't change the circumstances. She couldn't change past arguments or even how close they were physically. She wasn't going to move back to New York and become next door neighbors just so that they could work on the relationship.

Abigail started with the only thing she could change: her perspective. If she wanted things to be different, she had to change how she *thought* about her sister, which would help her change the *reality* of the relationship.

Now we're going to use Abigail's story to walk you through our perspective brainstorming exercise. When it's your turn to tackle one of your own disempowering stories, it can be helpful to do this exercise with at least one other person who you think could offer some objectivity (somebody who isn't directly involved), especially when the stakes are high. Whether you're doing it alone or with help, examine *all* the evidence, not just what you typically rely on to prove your perspective. Remember, we're often so entrenched in our stories, so sure that they're "the truth," that we can't see any possibility outside of them. This is a technique for fighting your way out of that trap and taking back the narratives that shape your life.

Steps 1–3: What is your disempowering story? What are the facts? What are the costs?

In the last chapter, we asked you to examine one of your own disempowering stories, distinguishing the facts from your perspective on those facts and becoming clear about the costs. This is a critical first step in choosing a new perspective because it encourages you to take a step back and try to think more objectively. The goal is to examine all the evidence, not just what you've used to build your story before. For instance, when you're doing this exercise, try to focus on things that people have *actually* said, written, or done, not what you believe they think or your interpretation of what they said. We began this section by describing the essential facts of Abigail's story and the cost of the story for her and her family.

Facts	Costs
• Leanne is Abigail's only sibling. • Leanne is three years younger. • They both have children and are married. • They live in different states.	• Abigail was sad to be missing an important relationship in her life. • Family gatherings could be tense. • The kids were missing out on a close relationship with their cousins.

Step 4: What is another perspective you could choose?

Once you have clarity about the facts and costs, you can begin brainstorming new, more empowering perspectives to rely on instead.

A perspective is not an action. It's an interpretation that reflects how we feel and think, not what we *do*. It's a lens through which we see the world. The goal of the exercise is to brainstorm and then choose a new lens for viewing the circumstances or relationship. **The ideas should not be actions or "solutions" to the problem, and they shouldn't be focused on trying to change other people or circumstances.** The person or people helping you brainstorm shouldn't be telling you what to do; they should be suggesting different ways of perceiving the situation.

If you're struggling to come up with possibilities, try these prompts:

- Consider the complete opposite of your perspective. This can be hard because you believe your story. Saying the opposite feels untrue because you have no evidence to support it. But remember, your current perspective isn't "the truth," either.

- How would you like the situation to look? How would you like to feel or what you would like to accomplish, as opposed to what's happening now? What story could you tell that would make that possible?

As people come up with ideas, somebody should record them, making sure to write down the current perspective first. You can use the perspective wheel in the downloadable workbook. Why a wheel? We wanted to emphasize that every perspective is equal to any other perspective. There is no "right" answer.

What are some alternative perspectives that Abigail could have adopted? The wheel on page 91 shows ideas she considered and that we've heard from others, but not nearly all of them, and not the one she ultimately chose.

Two important tips: First, it's important not to rationalize someone's behavior or confuse a perspective with empathy or compassion. In one of our sessions, somebody said, "Maybe Leanne doesn't like living in her older sister's shadow." If Abigail had adopted that perspective, how would it have changed anything? That said, choosing a new perspective often reduces the tendency to make judgments or assumptions, especially about other people, which makes room for empathy. Second, don't take your existing perspective, accept it as the truth, and then try to look on the bright side. For example, if your perspective is "My boss doesn't care about my career development," looking on the bright side might be, "I can always find another job or change teams." That won't help you think about or behave differently in the current situation. It's not empowering.

Once you have plenty of good possibilities in front of you, it's time to choose one. When choosing a new perspective, **choose the one that resonates with you most or that is most aligned with achieving your vision.**

Brainstorming Perspectives

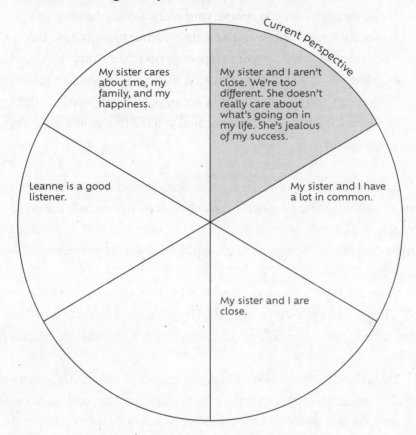

There's no one right answer. As long as the one you choose helps alleviate the costs, it will make a positive difference in your life. We encourage you to circle your choice. It creates a physical and visual reminder of the story you're trying to prove now.

Big, long-standing, emotional stories require big shifts to create change. So Abigail decided to start saying this to herself: "My sister and I are best friends." That might sound a little crazy, because it wasn't true from her perspective. It was a story she was making up. There was no evidence for it. *But the original story wasn't necessarily true either.*

Sometimes, when people hear this story, they ask, "Well, why wasn't it Leanne's responsibility to make things better?" Because Leanne wasn't

Brainstorming Perspectives

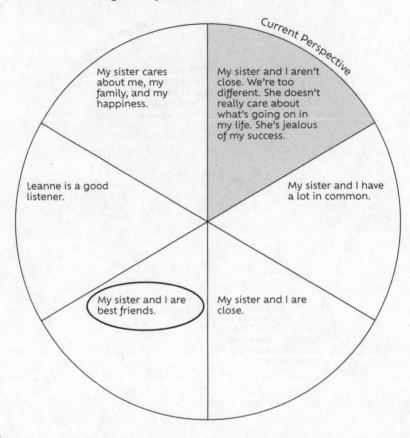

the one suffering. Well, maybe she was, but Abigail didn't know that. And trying to put the responsibility on Leanne wouldn't change anything for Abigail. If she wanted *her own* experience to change, she had to take 100 percent responsibility for the relationship.

Brainstorming new perspectives works equally well for stories about relationships and stories about situations. Recall Emma's story from the start of the chapter about her "up or out" promotion leading a new department. If she had been brainstorming possible perspectives with a friend or colleague, her perspective wheel might have looked something like the one shown here.

Brainstorming Perspectives

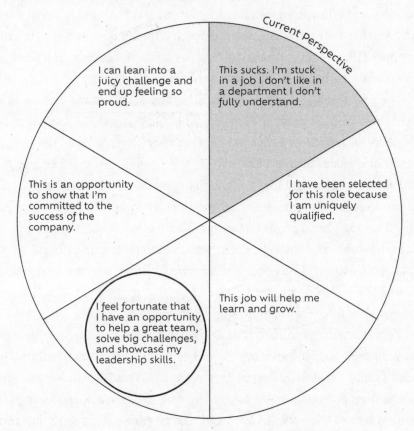

Step 5: *What will be different in how you think, speak, or act?*

Once you've chosen your new perspective, ask yourself this important reflective question: With this new lens, what will be different?

- How will you feel?
- How will your outlook be different in the future?
- What will you stop doing and start doing?
- What new ideas or possibilities might you consider that you would have shot down before?

The most important starting point is your language. Remember, reality is created and affirmed in your language. If you want to build belief in a *new* story, you have to stop telling the old one and find opportunities to tell the new one. This will feel awkward at first, as if you're faking it. You have no evidence for it—but over time, you'll collect that evidence.

The first thing Abigail had to ask herself was, "If Leanne was my best friend, how would I behave? What would I do differently?" Obviously, she wouldn't tell herself or other people that they weren't close. She would also be in regular contact with Leanne. She started with small changes in her behavior. She would text Leanne funny pictures of her kids or an article she thought she would find interesting. Then she stepped it up and started calling once a week. Sometimes Leanne would pick up and sometimes she wouldn't. When she did, it was awesome—because Abigail spoke to, laughed with, and responded to Leanne like they were best friends. A few months in, Abigail invited Leanne on a girls trip she was taking. Leanne said yes, and the trip was amazing.

That was years ago, and today, Abigail and Leanne *are* best friends. Their children and husbands are close. They spend vacations together. The entire family dynamic is better. Is it always perfect? Of course not. But with her new perspective, Abigail is more able to be patient and loving and compassionate. She's able to apologize and be transparent about her own missteps rather than being righteous, which creates the space for Leanne to do the same.

Abigail never told Leanne what she was doing or why—because it didn't matter. **What mattered was that she chose a new, more empowering perspective and took responsibility for their relationship.**

EXERCISE: CHOOSING YOUR NEW PERSPECTIVE

1. What is your disempowering story?
2. What are the facts?
3. What are the costs?
4. What is another perspective you could choose?
   - Consider asking somebody who can be objective to help you brainstorm.
   - Remember that a perspective is a way of thinking or feeling, not an action to take. Don't try to solve the problem.
   - Don't be limited by the current perspective — or try to rationalize, excuse, commiserate, or confirm the current perspective.
   - When the brainstorming is over, choose the new perspective that resonates most and physically circle it.
5. What will be different in how you think, speak, or act?

The more you practice choosing a new perspective, the better you'll get at it. You'll be able to do it with greater velocity, letting go of disempowering stories that are holding you back from the confidence, happiness, and resiliency that can make all the difference in life.

Chapter 7

FUEL YOUR OWN CONFIDENCE

During a recent program, one participant, Ethan, chose to share a negative story he had been telling himself with the group.

Ethan had gone to school for marketing and had worked on the same marketing team for six years. He'd risen through the ranks and was good at his job. One day, his manager shared a new company strategy: putting somebody with a marketing or sales background on the product development team. Ethan loved working with that team, especially on innovation and problem-solving, so he took a deep breath and went for it.

Ethan wanted to love his new role, to feel successful and confident, but most days he had a negative story running through his head: "I've made a huge mistake. I don't belong here. I don't have the right skill set for this. Everyone else has an engineering degree. *Why should they listen to me?*" Because of this perspective, he felt himself alternating between holding back when he had a (probably valuable) opinion or overcompensating and becoming domineering. He was also working long hours and volunteering for responsibilities that would be better handled by other people to "prove" himself. What he was describing was a classic example of imposter syndrome.

When he finished telling us his story, a colleague in the same group said, "I'm so surprised to hear you say that. You're the first person I go to when I have a question about our customers. Your knowledge of them has made every product you work on much better. Your work is proof that the new strategy is working. And you must be doing something right; you were just promoted." *Story versus fact.*

Some of the most negative stories we tell ourselves are the ones we tell about *ourselves.*

They can pop up at any moment, even when we're succeeding, and once they start, they often keep repeating on an automatic loop. They are about us *and* created by us, so there's often no external factor to counterbalance them, especially because we're usually too ashamed to admit to them. We call this type of story your *inner critic.*

Think about a moment just after you accomplished something and felt good or proud. Suddenly, some negative thought intruded. You started focusing on small missteps or things that didn't go exactly to plan. Your feeling of accomplishment was hijacked.

What is confidence? It's a feeling of self-assurance that comes when you appreciate your strengths, abilities, and qualities. You probably feel it in many parts of your life, but in others, you don't. Maybe you compare yourself to friends or colleagues or obsess over a perceived shortcoming. Maybe, like Ethan, you have imposter syndrome, worrying you don't have the experience or knowledge or capabilities to succeed. Or maybe, at the end of the day, instead of acknowledging what you *did* accomplish, you focus on what you didn't check off your lengthy to-do list. All of these unproductive, disempowering thoughts come from your inner critic and pull your focus away from appreciating your strengths, abilities, and qualities.

Your inner critic can increase your anxiety and stress, eat away at your enthusiasm and energy, and reduce your accomplishments. It can make you withdraw or hold back because you second-guess yourself, or overcompensate because you feel the need to prove yourself. When you put yourself in uncomfortable growth positions, your inner critic can get louder and more persistent. When you're stuck in a self-critical story, you can behave in ways that don't serve you or others and that limit your potential.

**Your inner critic reduces your power
to create the life you want.**

The good news is that you can manage your inner critic rather than letting it manage you. We've already given you an important strategy for doing so in the last chapter—choose a new perspective. It works for any recurring self-doubt or critical story. In this chapter, we're going to share more exercises to help you turn down the volume on your inner critic and mitigate its impact on your daily well-being. It's hard to completely shut that voice down, but with practice, you will recognize it faster and allow it to intrude less often.

Remember, the most important relationship you have is the one you have with yourself. Let's work on that relationship so you can feel proud of who you are and where you are in your life, right now. When you feel confident and optimistic, you'll have more capacity to contribute to the people and projects you care about most, you'll be better prepared to take on new challenges, and you'll create the life you want sooner rather than later.

THE ROOMMATE YOU WOULD NEVER CHOOSE

We sometimes refer to the inner critic as the roommate you would never choose, but who's always there—harsh and critical, ready to pounce in your most vulnerable moments. Once it starts, it can become a rant, like this one:

I can't believe I didn't work out this morning. I keep setting my alarm and then I just turn it off. I need to be more disciplined. My house is a total mess. I just have no discipline. Yesterday I was late for that meeting, but everybody else got there on time. I should have left ten minutes earlier. I am so overwhelmed, and I keep saying yes to everyone, and then I let everyone down, and I'm always late and behind. I just have to be more disciplined.

Does this sound familiar? We all have internal thoughts like these in certain situations or with certain people. We would never speak this way to other people, and yet we're all too comfortable speaking like this to ourselves.

One of our participants, Talia, had a strong inner critic. The core message of her negative monologue was, "I'm not good enough." Consequently, she believed she didn't deserve the good things that came her way or the things she really wanted in her life: a certain position at work, time to focus on her family, and especially fulfilling relationships.

Her new social circle was a perfect example. One of her best friends, Jane, had introduced Talia to the group. At first, she felt grateful. They were influential people in the community, and they all seemed to lead exciting lives. Every time she left a social gathering, though, a familiar loop would start. *I can't believe I said that. Sara was obviously annoyed. I'm so out of the loop. They all noticed I hadn't seen the documentary they were talking about. I can't believe I wore this old dress. Veronica called it "my favorite." She obviously noticed I wore it last month. This is why Joe didn't invite me to his happy hour last week—no one really wanted me there.* Her inner critic was convincing her that if she wasn't feeling comfortable, confident, and welcome in this group, *she* was the problem.

After using some of the practices we share in this chapter to recognize her inner critic, Talia began to turn down the volume and take actions to fuel her confidence. By focusing on her history of showing up as a caring friend, she could acknowledge that she deserved relationships that made her feel fulfilled and valued. When she could look at the situation more objectively, she realized her new social circle didn't offer that and wasn't aligned with her values. She gave herself permission to invest her time and energy elsewhere and has been happier ever since.

Our inner critic can be harsh and irrational. It can keep us up at night and tear us down. The first important step Talia took was to become conscious of her inner critic. You can do the same.

When we do this next exercise with groups, we tell people in advance, "You may not like this." We still do it because it makes such a difference in people's lives. People have told us that writing down what their inner critic says helps them recognize how harsh and irrational they can be. They can acknowledge that most of their negative thoughts aren't true and even seem absurd once they get them on paper. They realize how sad it is that they think these things, and that they would never speak this way to other people.

It may feel uncomfortable, but getting up close and personal with your inner critic is how you lessen its intensity, power, and impact in your life.

EXERCISE: GET TO KNOW YOUR INNER CRITIC

- Take a few minutes to think about circumstances, areas of your life, or relationships in which you feel less confident or as if you're falling short. Write down all the things your inner critic says, without editing yourself or holding back.
- How did it feel to write them down? How does it feel to see them on the page?
- Find somebody you trust and ask them to listen without trying to comfort you or convince you that you're wrong. Read your list out loud to them. How does it feel? Do these things seem irrational, sad, or harsh when you say them aloud?

- Reflect—would you say any of these things to somebody you cared about? If not, isn't it time to stop saying them to yourself?

You Don't Need Your Inner Critic to Motivate You

Some people believe that their inner critic is the source of their success, the voice pushing them to grow and improve.

When we rely on our inner critic, we're following a stressful rather than fulfilling path to the things we want to achieve. In their book *Above the Line*, neuropsychologist Mara Klemich and Stephen Klemich explain that we have two choices in how we operate day to day and moment to moment: above the line with effective, growth-oriented behaviors or below the line with dysfunctional, self-limiting behaviors. When we're operating below the line, we're driven to achieve by our inner critic—out of our fear of rejection and the need to prove ourselves. We're living "*for* significance—seeking our worth from our external environment by proving, performing, and perfecting."[1] But when we're operating above the line, we're driven to continuously and courageously improve by our sense of purpose and our desire for authentic personal growth. "We live *from* significance—our inner worth and value." In their research with more than a hundred thousand people, the Klemichs found that people who scored above the line in their thinking and behaviors reported "high levels of happiness and effectiveness at work, high-quality relationships, and low levels of stress."

Rational, purpose-driven, continuous efforts toward improvement and growth

---

Irrational, fear-driven, stressful attempts to prove our worth

You don't need an inner critic to grow and improve and achieve your goals. It's not constructive, and it's not rational. And trying to leverage it will limit your peace, your happiness, and your potential. Instead, learn to manage it so that you can focus on above-the-line growth and achievement.

4 PRACTICES TO MANAGE YOUR INNER CRITIC

Practice 1: Focus on Your Strengths

More than two decades ago, Gallup began publishing a series of books based on their deep research into strengths-based working, living, parenting, and leading. Through hundreds of thousands of assessments and roughly two million interviews, they proved one idea again and again: When we understand our strengths and apply them, we are more productive and effective and have a better quality of life—characterized by "having ample energy, feeling well-rested, being happy, smiling or laughing a lot, learning something interesting."[2] VIA Institute on Character uses the term "character strengths" to define these core, positive aspects of identity. Their research shows that when we leverage our character strengths, we boost our confidence, strengthen our relationships, navigate problems more successfully, reduce our stress, and find meaning and purpose.

Remember, confidence and self-assurance come from appreciating your strengths, abilities, and qualities. Unfortunately, we aren't very good at doing this. Instead, we tend to rely on other people to do it for us. It would be so great if we all had people running after us to tell us how awesome we were in that meeting or how much they loved our ideas or how we're killing it as a parent or friend, but that's not realistic. You can't count on other people to fuel your confidence.

You can fuel your confidence by acknowledging your *own* strengths — rather than waiting for somebody else to do it for you.

You can begin to fuel your confidence by recognizing what you're good at, your best qualities, and what's working for you and then putting those things to use as often as possible. That's what the next exercise is all about.

EXERCISE: FOCUS ON YOUR STRENGTHS

1. Take a look at the chart on pages 106–107. Circle your top three to five strengths (as perceived by you!).
2. Where are you currently using your strengths?
3. How else could you leverage your strengths in your life, work, and relationships? (For example, if one of your strengths is creativity, but you don't feel that your current role requires creative work, could you leverage your creative thinking within that role anyway to innovatively solve a challenge or improve a product or service?)

Another way to focus on your strengths is to graciously accept compliments and praise. If you are deflecting or disagreeing, *stop*. Accept that you deserve it. Take it in and say, "Thank you."

Practice 2: Run Your Own Race

Isaac was ambitious. He was ready to move up, ready to accelerate his career growth. There was just one problem: He knew he wasn't the only talented team member eyeing the next open position. *I just need to prove myself*, he thought.

This mindset opened the door for his inner critic, which was loudest when Isaac wasn't invited to certain meetings and his colleagues were. *Why did that person get invited? Why wasn't I? What did I do? They're going to move up faster than I am. Maybe I'm not that good in client meetings.* He started keeping a mental record of which colleagues were invited to which meetings and how much face time they were getting with the manager. He became convinced that there was no way he was going to get promoted because other people were getting more exposure. His mood at work shifted. Finally, his manager brought it up during a one-on-one meeting. She had noticed a change in his attitude and his work.

This is where things stood when we met Isaac. We could see how desperately he needed to shut down his inner critic and *run his own race*. If he couldn't, it might create a self-fulfilling prophecy.

Thoroughbred horses on a racetrack wear blinders. Their trainers put the blinders on to keep the horses from being distracted by the other horses on either side. It helps them stay focused on what's in front of them and on running their own best race. Humans are the same. If we don't take precautions, we can easily get distracted from our own goals and contributions by the behaviors and accomplishments of the people around us.

The inner critic likes to point out that others are smarter, more successful, more attractive, better parents, have nicer homes, take nicer vacations, have more friends, make more money, are further along in their careers, and on and on. With every comparison, it diminishes our own accomplishments and contributions. Social media, both personal and professional, is one of the biggest triggers. Multiple studies have shown just how quickly even a brief exposure to social media can sink our self-esteem—all because of our "upward social comparisons."[3]

As if constant comparison isn't enough, we're also hyper-focused on what other people think of us. We're social creatures, and we want to be liked and included. We worry about it so much that it affects our judgment, decisions, and behaviors. We avoid conflict. We don't ask for help because we don't want people to think we're not capable. We don't share opinions that we think might be unpopular.

It's incredibly difficult to eliminate comparison from your thinking and to stop worrying about what other people think of you. But raising your consciousness of where these things are *dominating* your thinking and holding you back can help you identify their triggers, reduce their impact, and spend more time focused on your strengths and contributions.

That's the work that Isaac did. As soon as he recognized the cost of his incessant comparison (well-being, work relationships, and productivity), he was able to shift his focus. He assessed his strengths and focused on his contributions and successes with clients. He stopped checking the calendar for client meetings that weren't his. He vulnerably discussed

Strengths You May Have

Creativity Original, adaptive, a problem solver, sees and does things in different ways	**Curiosity** Interested, explores new things, open to new ideas
Perspective Wise, provides good counsel, takes the big picture view	**Bravery** Shows valor, doesn't shrink from fear, speaks up for what's right
Zest Enthusiastic, energetic, doesn't do things half-heartedly	**Love** Warm and genuine, values close relationships
Teamwork Team player, socially responsible, loyal	**Fairness** Just, doesn't let feelings bias decisions about others
Humility Modest, lets one's accomplishments speak for themselves	**Prudence** Careful, cautious, takes appropriate risk
Gratitude Thankful for good things, expresses thanks, feels fortunate	**Hope** Optimistic, future-minded

Judgment A critical thinker, thinks things through, open-minded	**Love of Learning** Masters new skills and topics, systematically adds to knowledge
Perseverance Persistent, industrious, finishes what one starts	**Honesty** Authentic, trustworthy, sincere
Kindness Generous, nurturing, caring, compassionate, altruistic	**Social intelligence** Aware of the motives and feelings of others, knows what makes others tick
Leadership Organizes group activities to get things done, positively influences others	**Forgiveness** Merciful, accepts others' shortcomings, gives people a second chance
Self-regulation Self-controlled, manages impulses and emotions	**Appreciation of beauty & excellence** Feels awe and wonder in beauty, inspired by goodness of others
Humor Playful, brings smiles to others, lighthearted	**Spirituality** Searches for meaning, feels a sense of purpose, senses a relationship with something beyond oneself

his challenges and his career goals with his manager, who gave him great coaching and positive feedback and appreciated his openness. Isaac felt like he was growing, improving, and contributing to the team. He said it felt like such a relief, and he was much happier and more productive.

EXERCISE: RUN YOUR OWN RACE

- Where in your life are you feeling triggered by comparing yourself to others? (Consider your career, your relationships, your home, your health and body image, and more.) What do you say to yourself?
- Where in your life are you overly focused on what other people think of you rather than what you know you have to offer? What does that cost you?
- What can you stop doing or start doing to run your own race and focus on your own contributions? (For example, reduce time on social media, shift from envy to admiration and curiosity, create reminders of your own vision and priorities.)

Practice 3: A 2.5 Minute Journaling Practice

Yes, we know you've been told to journal before—*and* we know that you probably aren't doing it. Most people don't, despite the massive benefits. It combats depression. It boosts your self-esteem and self-awareness. It improves relationships. It helps you process difficult experiences. It even boosts your immune system and your IQ![4] In one study, older people who were asked to write about an emotional experience for just twenty minutes for three consecutive days were almost *twice* as likely to heal quickly after a surgical procedure.[5]

The amazing thing about journaling is that doing even a minimal amount can make a big difference. We're going to give you an easy, effective, and fast journaling technique to convince you that you *can* make time for it. The key is to focus your brain on your strengths, abilities, and qualities and to nurture a positive outlook. You don't have to overthink it. It's more important to do it consistently than to be deep and thoughtful about everything you write down. Be honest and earnest.

EXERCISE: JOURNAL IN THE MORNING AND EVENING

- Morning: Write down two or three things you are grateful for today.
  For example: my delicious cup of coffee, my partner's support, my cold shower after exercising, this mild weather, my kid's hug before school
- Evening: Write down two or three things you are proud of or did well in the last twenty-four hours.
  For example: I contributed to my retirement account, I spoke up in our monthly meeting, I called a friend I haven't seen in a while, I helped my daughter with her homework, I forgave a friend, I helped a frazzled coworker with an important project.

Practice 4: Clear Power Outages

We bet that at some point in the last month, you had a moment of rant-inducing anger, swirling angst and self-doubt, or just a total lack of motivation that put you into a downward spiral. You were going through life feeling good when suddenly something happened—you mishandled a situation or made a mistake, someone failed to deliver or gave you negative feedback, or something just didn't work out as you expected or hoped. And in that moment, the clouds rolled in, lightning struck, and you had what we call a "power outage."

We call these moments power outages because you have a sudden loss of power. You feel like you're stuck in the dark! You might feel helpless, out of control, or unable to move forward. Some power outages are minor and some are major. Big or small, they are inevitable, a result of being human in a human world, putting yourself in uncomfortable growth positions, and working toward your bold vision (and sometimes failing). The key is learning how to get out of a power outage quickly so you can get back to your life!

You can usually tell you're in a power outage when you're obsessing about something and can't seem to move past it. You might even have a physical response. Here are some of the common signs.

- Obsessing over a particular moment, interaction, or situation
- Feeling distracted and unable to focus
- Feeling frustration, anger, irritation, guilt, or depression
- Lacking energy and motivation
- A physical stress response, like sweaty palms, shaky hands, clenched jaw, or crying

Our brains process social or psychological needs and threats in essentially the same way they process physical needs and threats.[6] When you're in a power outage, your threat response has kicked in. Your executive functioning takes a hit and your inner critic or disempowering stories aren't tamped down by calmer, more rational thinking. They're free to run wild. You're suddenly listing the ten things you should have done or said instead, the twelve pieces of evidence that somebody is an idiot, and all the signs that you're heading for a catastrophe. If you're not careful, you can make some unwise decisions (like sending an email that should *definitely not* be sent).

The good news is that power outages are temporary. As one of our participants said, "At ten o'clock it's the worst thing in the world. You want everybody fired or you're drafting irate emails. And then two hours later you're asking, 'So, what's for lunch?'"

The best thing you can do is learn to clear power outages so you can have fewer of them and spend less time in them.

Here's an example of what our technique looks like in action.

Lisa: A few years ago, I wrote and rewrote a sensitive email to a few people on our team giving direction on repairing a relationship and process with a client. I pressed send and then my heart stopped. I realized I had inadvertently copied the client on the email. I started to sweat. I couldn't think. My mind was racing. So I called Wendy and said, "I'm having a major power outage." This is how she helped me clear it.

Wendy:	"What's going on?"
Me:	"I sent an internal, sensitive email to a client by accident. I'm mortified. How could I do this? I was moving too fast. I'm beyond embarrassed."
Wendy:	"Got it. Tell me more about it."
Me:	"You would think at this point in my career I wouldn't make these kinds of mistakes. I feel like I let the team down. I'm so mad at myself. How could I do this?!"
Wendy:	"I really get it. Anything else you want to say about it?"
Me:	"No. That's it."
Wendy:	"Is there anything you think you should do about this today?"
Me:	"I plan to apologize both to the team and the client. I'll call my people and send the client a note."
Wendy:	"Sounds great. You still seem pretty mad at yourself right now. When will you forgive yourself?"
Me:	"You're right, I am. I need a little time. I will forgive myself by the time I go to bed tonight."
Wendy:	"OK. How do you feel now?"

Me: "Still a little embarrassed, but better, calmer. Thank you!"

What Wendy did was **listen without interrupting, without judgment, without trying to console, and without trying to fix the problem.** None of that would have been helpful because Lisa was too busy beating herself up. Wendy helped her get all the angst out and reset so that she could focus on next steps. You can find somebody to help you clear power outages, and you can help others, too!

A GUIDE TO CLEARING YOUR POWER OUTAGES

- **Step 1: Recognize that you're in a power outage.** Think about a recent power outage or two, then answer these questions: What does a power outage usually look like for you? What kinds of situations trigger them? What does your inner critic say? What happens for you physically? What types of things do you typically say or do when you're in a power outage? Use your answers to help you recognize that you're in a power outage the next time.
- **Step 2: Breathe.** Taking deep breaths helps calm our stress response, so start there.
- **Step 3: Don't stay alone.** Identify one or two people in your life who you can turn to, meaning you're comfortable being vulnerable and not "perfect" with them. Their role is to help you purge the negative thoughts and reset. It could be a friend, a sibling, or your spouse. Their task is easy: Listen and ask a couple of questions. Before your next power outage, give them these guidelines:

- They should listen without interrupting. If you stop talking, they should say something like, "What else?" or "Tell me more" or "Is there anything else you want to say?"
- When you're done, they should not commiserate, try to solve your problem, or tell you what you should do.
- If your power outage is because of your own mistake or somebody else's, they might ask, "When will you let this go? When will you forgive yourself/them?" You should set a timeline because it takes time to move past anger or disappointment.
- They can ask questions to help you reset your thinking and focus on moving forward, such as, "What do you think you should do now/next/today?"
- When it seems like you're refocused, they can ask, "How do you feel now?" to make sure that the power outage is over.

When you're in a power outage, saying what you're thinking and feeling out loud tends to neutralize the drama and heat, but sometimes all it takes is slowing down, getting present, and being intentional about resetting your thinking and your perspective. That's a good starting point if you can't find somebody to help you clear it. It's a simple practice, but it makes a massive difference in terms of how much of your life you spend feeling angry, frustrated, guilty, low, or unconfident.

It's *so* easy to become resigned to living with this roommate you would never choose, to stop recognizing how critical they are and how much they influence your happiness and especially your confidence. That's not the way it has to be. Which of these practices will you commit to? Start managing your inner critic and fighting back! It will take practice, but it's worth it. Fueling your own confidence will improve the most crucial relationship you have in your life: the one with yourself. The greater your confidence, the greater your ability to create the life you want.

PLAN THE WORK AND WORK THE PLAN

Start Taking Ground — Today

Chapter 8

TAKING CONTROL OF YOUR TIME, ENERGY, AND FOCUS

At least once a week, we hear somebody shift from excitement to resignation in the space of a minute. The excitement comes as they read their vision out loud. Then they pause, their face falls a little, and they share one of the most universal limiting beliefs (and a chief excuse for not pursuing our goals): "I have no idea how I'm going to do this. I don't have the time or energy."

At one workshop, we heard these words from a leader named Darius. He then spent five minutes talking about all the things that would get in the way of "finding" the time, energy, and focus to work on his important outcomes for the year. His work calendar was public, and people at his company could just pop meetings onto it. He spent his days jumping from meeting to meeting and trying to get important tasks accomplished early in the morning or late at night. He was in a client-facing role, and if a client called or messaged—even if it was after hours—he always answered. At

117

home, his kid's activities took up evenings and weekends. He and his wife hadn't been on a date in four months.

He wrapped up with a statement we've heard from many people over the years: "My calendar is not my own." Other people in the room nodded vigorously.

"If it's not yours," we asked, "*whose is it?*"

We *think* we don't have the power to control how we spend our time or where we direct our energy and focus, so we give up that power. We spend our days being *reactive* rather than *intentional*, just responding to the needs, priorities, demands, and crises that come at us rather than making progress on our own priorities. We end up feeling like there aren't enough hours in the day and that other people and circumstances dictate how we use the time we *do* have. We often feel unproductive or incapable of achieving our goals—professional or personal. In the words of Jim Kwik, author and "brain coach," "Sometimes you're burnt out not because you're doing too much but because you're doing too little of the things that make you come alive."[1]

>>

Your reactive behaviors can and will derail you from achieving your vision and creating the life you want.

>>

The first step to making sure that doesn't happen is *recognizing where and when* you are being reactive. Take a minute right now to think about an area of your life where things are working—where things feel easy, low-stress, and within your control, whether you're onboarding a new client, planning your next vacation, or exercising. You know what you need to do and you do it, without friction. This is likely an area of your life where you are intentional.

Now think about situations or circumstances where you feel the opposite, as if every step is a struggle or like you're running in circles and making no progress. Maybe you find yourself getting emotionally hooked, feeling frustrated or even guilty. You might complain about it to other people or in your own head. Whatever it is, you feel like it's somehow out of your control, as if you're operating on autopilot. Maybe one these scenarios sounds familiar.

- Obsessively checking email or text messages (especially if you have notifications turned on)
- Staying up late bingeing TV shows, getting sucked into social media, or doomscrolling on a news site (there's an actual phrase for doing this after overly packed days: revenge bedtime procrastination)
- Holding onto tasks that could be delegated because "it's just easier"
- Saying yes to drinks or dinner out when you're trying to be healthy or save money
- Agreeing to social or community commitments because you think you're "supposed to," not because they're meaningful to you
- Spending time solving other people's problems or helping them achieve their goals and then feeling resentful because you have no energy left for your own

It doesn't have to be this way. You can choose to be intentional and focus on what you *can* control rather than reacting to what you can't. In the rest of this chapter, we'll help you become conscious of where you're being reactive, examine the costs, and identify new habits and behaviors that will help you be intentional.

That's what we helped Darius do. With a better understanding of the cost of his reactive behaviors, he came up with new habits. He began reviewing his calendar two weeks out to identify meetings that were not a valuable use of his time, and then he asked the meeting owners whether it was important for him to attend. Most said it wasn't. He also blocked two mornings a week in his calendar as "unavailable" to make time for strategic projects and to give him time to think. At home, he talked to his wife about alternating attendance at less important kid events—an idea she was thrilled about. They put a regular date night on the calendar every month and he joined a weekly tennis clinic. With simple, immediate actions, Darius took control of his calendar and life and "found" time and energy to devote to outcomes in his bold vision—and to have some fun!

You can become more focused, productive, and lit up by the things you spend time on. The shift begins when you choose to be intentional.

NOT MORE, DIFFERENT

I have enough time and energy for the things that are most important to me.

Does that sound like a fantasy? Most of us think that to achieve more of what we want we need *more* time and energy because we need to *do* more. We have to squeeze in one more call or accomplish one more task. What if you could *do less* and *accomplish more*? That's what happens when you adopt this empowering perspective. You begin to see that you don't need more time, you need to choose to do *different* things with the time you have.

Right now, in your life, you're probably spending time on things that aren't mission critical, that aren't in service of your vision, and that don't fuel your success, happiness, or peace. They stem from reactive, autopilot behaviors, like saying yes when you want to say no. (We'll offer coaching and language in chapter ten to help you become comfortable and confident saying no.) In *Essentialism*, a book about achieving more while doing less, Greg McKeown writes, "Everything changes when we give ourselves permission to be more selective in what we choose to do . . . There is tremendous freedom in learning that we can eliminate the non-essentials, that we are no longer controlled by other people's agendas, and that we get to choose."[2]

Those words *permission* and *freedom* are key. Most of us, in some area of our lives, are waiting for others to give us permission to make a different choice about our time and our priorities. Have you ever stayed at work late because your colleagues were still there, even though you'd made another commitment? Have you ever needed to take a sick day but didn't because you were worried about how it might look to your team or your manager? Have you ever wanted to just sit and read, but you didn't want your partner to feel you weren't handling your share of responsibilities around the house? We once had a participant share, "I wish every day felt like Saturday." When we asked what he meant by that, he said, "Just the freedom of not being on somebody else's timeline or always waiting for the next crisis or meeting to crop up."

When you stop *waiting* for permission and give yourself permission instead, you will find freedom—freedom of choice, freedom from others' agendas, and freedom to do the things that are most important. Being intentional takes rigor and discipline, *and* it gives us the freedom to prioritize what we want and need. "It allows you to cut out all of the extraneous BS in life that leads you nowhere," somebody in a workshop said. "Planning your time can sound like a little 'discipline prison,' but in fact it's incredibly freeing." For example, Wendy loves to walk. It helps her feel healthier and more energized, it gives her time to think, and she gets to spend time with her pups. She puts that time on her calendar every day. Knowing it's there removes the nagging worry that it might not happen and gives her a sense of freedom in how she spends her time.

Laura Vanderkam, speaker and author of books like *Tranquility by Tuesday* and *168 Hours*, has researched this idea deeply. She guided people to add activities to their schedules that aligned with their priorities—especially things that fed adventure, replenishment, connection, and health. Even though she *didn't* ask them to cut anything out to make time for the new things, they reported feeling happier *and less time-starved*. "When life is full of have-to-dos, with only brief periods of downtime in between, we can feel beaten down by responsibilities. But add things we actually want to do, to compete with those have-to-dos, and time feels different."[3] **Saying yes to**

something, like commitments in your bold vision, is more motivating than saying no to something.

Building more intentional habits that support your goals *also* helps you shed those tasks and responsibilities that aren't meaningful or that aren't a good use of your unique talents or competencies. Take Ava, whose biggest struggle was delegation. She worked for a fast-growth company and had been there from the beginning. When the company was small, everybody was expected to swim in ten different lanes and say yes to whatever needed to be done. The company was now worth billions, had more than twenty thousand employees, and work had been parsed out across several new departments. But Ava's mindset about her work *hadn't* changed as dramatically as the company. Her reactive, autopilot behavior was to handle whatever needed to be handled, without asking if she was the right person to handle it. Her days were loaded with tasks that could have been accomplished by other people, eating up time and energy she could have invested in more strategic work. For instance, in her vision, she had written that she was spending time coaching her team every week but was struggling to make that happen.

One day, she was frantically building a presentation, trying to get video elements to work, when a colleague came in to ask her a question. When she told him how frustrated she was, he asked, "Did you ask creative services for help?" Of course she hadn't, even though they were the people expected to help with this exact task. "It was a wake-up call," she told us. "I was looking for time to spend with my team, and there it was. I had spent ninety minutes doing something that I didn't have to do." Ava began noticing all the ways she didn't tap into the resources, knowledge, and talent available to her. Within a couple of months, she had "found" five or six hours a week, which she devoted to work that was important and that made her feel competent and successful.

Small, intentional choices and behaviors create space and allow you to feel more confident and fulfilled. Over time, you achieve more without doing more.

TAKING CONTROL

Our three-question exercise will help you take control of your focus, energy, and time by identifying where you're being reactive, getting clear about the costs, and committing to new behaviors or habits. From there, it just takes practice to start reaping the benefits.

1. Identify an area in your life where you are being reactive. What is the automatic behavior or pattern?

> **Wendy:** For years, I was addicted to my phone, responding to any notification that came through. If it vibrated, buzzed, or lit up, I *had* to grab it. It didn't matter what I was doing at the time—talking with a coworker, eating dinner with my husband, Gary, or reading a great book. I could be watching an engrossing movie with my family at nine o'clock at night, and I would *still* grab for it the moment it dinged. It was a physical, Pavlovian response, and a classic example of reactive, autopilot behavior.
>
> One night a few years ago, Gary was telling me an important story about something that had happened at work when my phone buzzed and I picked it up. "I'm sitting right here," he said, clearly frustrated and angry. "Could you pay attention to me please?" It was the first time I began to truly recognize the cost of the behavior, and that I was doing it *all the time.*
>
> That moment, and the resulting conversation with Gary, forced me to acknowledge that it was time to take control.

Wendy's story is common these days, but as we've described, this type of reactive behavior shows up throughout our lives. Technology doesn't help, but it's not the only trigger. As you consider where in your life you're being reactive, look back at the examples we shared at the beginning of the chapter or think about an area of your life where you feel out of control, unproductive, or stressed. You may come up with more than one example—or more than ten (many people do). If you're struggling to figure out which one to start working on, choose the one that has you thinking, *This is definitely going to get in the way of me achieving my vision.*

2. What are the costs of this behavior to you and others?

Acknowledging the costs of our behaviors can motivate us to change. Gary helped Wendy wake up to the costs of her phone addiction, but to change, she knew she would need to go deeper. She spent time thinking about how other people perceived her behavior and realized that they probably felt her phone was more important than they were in the moment. She was less present in all parts of her life because a part of her brain was always waiting for the next notification. She also had to acknowledge the cost to her own sense of peace. She felt that she had to be on and responding all the time. Acknowledging those costs motivated her to develop better habits for being intentional with her focus.

If possible, you should work on this question and the next with another person. As Gary did, they can share how a behavior affects them or other people in your life, or they can offer another perspective. Common costs to consider are negative impacts on your productivity, sleep, confidence, sense of accomplishment, and connection with others. If you need help digging in, consider these questions:

- Do you lose patience with your colleagues or your family?
- Do you miss or forget important details of conversations and meetings?
- Are you often late or do you miss deadlines?
- Do people "joke" with you about a certain behavior, but you feel like they're trying to tell you something?
- Do you feel regret or guilt at the end of the day or week about things you didn't accomplish?

- Do you carry a sense of shame or embarrassment about long-standing goals that you can't seem to accomplish?
- Do you look at your to-do list or calendar and feel completely overwhelmed?

3. What two or three new behaviors or habits could help you be intentional?

Do you remember Avery from the first pages of the book? She was living an overwhelmed, reactive life as a leader who also had a baby. Her life wasn't working for her, and in every coaching session, Wendy asked her, "*What could you do about it?*" That's the big question here. What could you do differently to feel more in control, to give yourself permission and freedom? Remember, you have the power to make different choices.

The more specific you can be, especially about the frequency or timing of the new habit or behavior, the better. If you're vague, it's easy to let yourself off the hook. For instance, if you're trying to build a new habit to break away from reactive eating, saying, "I'm going to eat healthier" won't get you far. You *could* track and hold yourself accountable to "I'm not going to buy any snack foods this month." Saying, "I'm going to spend less time in meetings" won't have as much impact as saying, "Before agreeing to attend a meeting, I'm going to ask, 'What's my role?' to determine whether I need to be there."

Identify two or three things you could *start doing* and *keep doing* that would make a difference. Again, asking another person to help you brainstorm strategies or new habits can be helpful. You might come up with a long list, but you should focus on just a few so that you can start building a new habit without feeling like you have to change everything all at once. Once you've decided where to start, tell other people what you plan to do and ask them to hold you accountable. In the workbook available at FastForwardGroup.net/Book, we offer plenty of examples and additional tips for owning your time.

Wendy knew she had to get a handle on her behavior, so set new habits to establish boundaries and guardrails. During dinner, she put her phone in a basket by the front door. When she was in meetings, she put it away. On the weekends and in the mornings, she created "no phone zones," blocking time to focus entirely on important things, like family, work that required deep focus, or just relaxation. She also scheduled time to respond to emails. She asked people to hold her accountable, especially Gary, her kids, and Lisa. None of these strategies were rocket science, but it didn't occur to her to even try to change until she snapped out of autopilot and thought about the costs of being so reactive.

We're not exaggerating when we say that the results were life-changing. Her relationships were deeper, and the time she spent with people was more fulfilling. She was present and listening, people felt heard, and she learned things she had been missing. She was more productive and felt calmer and more in control. She's not perfect, and sometimes she gets off-track. After a setback, she lets it go, resets, and commits to being intentional the next day.

Will your efforts play out exactly as you intend, all the time? Probably not. Things will crop up that derail you: fire alarms, last minute requests, sudden changes in plans. With a plan for being intentional, you'll go into each day with a mindset and perspective of ownership and control, and that will help you get back on track. We've had so many workshop participants share that with attention and intention, they were able to make a huge improvement in a short amount of time.

EXERCISE: SHIFTING FROM REACTIVE TO INTENTIONAL

1. Identify one area in your life where you're being reactive. What is the automatic behavior or pattern?
2. What are the costs of this behavior for you and others?
3. What are two or three new behaviors or habits that could help you be intentional?

You can choose to tell yourself an empowering story about your time, energy, and focus—that you have enough and that you get to choose how you use it. This perspective can become your *reality* when you shift from being reactive to being intentional. We encouraged you to take the first steps in this chapter: recognizing where you're being reactive, identifying the costs, and brainstorming ideas for new behaviors. What new practice or habit have you committed to? The next step is to cement new behaviors *and* use your "found" time and energy to take action on your vision. In the next chapter, we'll show you how by creating a realistic action plan for your next ninety days.

Chapter 9

A PLAN THAT GIVES YOU MOTIVATION AND MOMENTUM

Gabriel held a high-pressure job that he loved, but he felt it was taking a toll on his relationship with his two kids, Elliott and Maddie, ages seven and nine. He wasn't as close and connected with them as he wanted to be, and he recognized that these were important years in their lives. He would hear his wife reference some inside joke or offer some guidance on an argument with a friend and feel jealous—*not* how anybody wants to feel about their spouse being a great parent. She took the lead with the kids, and he found himself unsure how to play a bigger role in the family dynamic.

In his vision, Gabriel had set professional and personal outcomes, but the quality of his relationship with his kids was top of mind. In his vision, he wrote, *Elliott and Maddie feel that I am present and interested in their lives. I spend one-on-one time with each of them weekly and we are deeply connected, aware of the small but important things in each other's lives. We are making memories.*

When Wendy met with him to discuss how he was taking ground each month, what she found is that he *wasn't*, at least not on that outcome. He said he felt stuck. "Honestly, I'm not sure how to make it happen."

"What's one thing you could do now that could make a difference?"

"I could spend more time with them."

That statement perfectly captures the challenge so many of us face when it comes to taking ground on our visions. "Things rarely get stuck because of lack of time," writes David Allen in *Getting Things Done*. "They get stuck because what 'doing' would look like, and where it happens, hasn't been decided . . . The real problem is a lack of clarity and definition."[1] Most of us can relate. We have good intentions, but only a vague sense of what to *do*. We aren't sure how to start. Sometimes we start but then aren't sure where to go next, or we get overwhelmed by too many choices and don't follow through.

Without a plan, you're lost in the woods without a compass. You're a busy person with a to-do list, reacting rather than being intentional, and not taking ground on your goals. You're *hoping* the future will turn out as you want, but **hope is not a strategy.**

——————————— » ———————————

The solution is to create a 90-day action plan that helps you focus on small, actionable, specific steps to achieve important outcomes in your vision.

——————————— » ———————————

Our 90-Day Action Plan can help you bridge the gap between knowing and doing, or what psychologists call the intention-behavior gap. You know what you want to do, but you either aren't doing it or aren't sure what *specific* actions to take to make progress. A plan helps you approach your outcomes step-by-step, discovering the path of least resistance to the future you want. It enables you to track your progress, gives you a sense of accomplishment that feeds your motivation, and helps you become more intentional with your time, energy, and focus.

That's what Wendy helped Gabriel do. "Let's get specific," she said. "Let's work backward from the outcome to where you are today. What are a few things you could do now that would move the needle? *How* could you spend more time with them?"

He gave this a little thought and even pulled up the family calendar. "Maddie's Girl Scouts troop does a lot of camping and outdoor activities. My wife isn't a fan, but I am. I could take over those activities with Maddie. There's a big hike in two weeks."

"Great. What about Elliott?"

"He loves reading, and he's just old enough for the Harry Potter series. I could read those books to him. We could start this week."

Gabriel gave himself the gift of two clear actions that he could take almost immediately. They helped him feel optimistic rather than stuck. The next time we checked in, he said, "It's been amazing. Maddie and I are having so much fun on the Girl Scouts trips, and the shared experiences we have give us stuff to talk about. I've met other dads in the group, too. Elliott and I have made it through the first two books, and we went to a Harry Potter event at the children's museum." Month by month, Gabriel was intentional in working toward his outcome, focusing on specific actions he could take to build his connection with his kids. Years later, he is still posting online about their fun adventures, like a white water rafting trip with Maddie and a trip to New York to see a show on Broadway with Elliott.

In this chapter, we'll help you solve the problem David Allen described so that you can start taking ground on your vision *now*, like Gabriel did. We'll help you **create a plan that becomes an active dashboard guiding you toward the life you want.** It will have three characteristics:

- Outcome-based: You'll start with the finish, focusing on specific outcomes from your vision and gathering evidence that they're possible as you go.
- Simple: You'll focus on a few achievable actions or habits that will make a difference now and bring you closer to your outcome.

- Concrete: You'll get highly specific so that you know exactly what you should be working on, and you'll set deadlines for actions and a frequency for habits.

The focus on outcomes is key. We'll help you prioritize a few outcomes from your vision and then work back to where you are right now to consider the next logical step forward. That's why we call it reverse engineering your vision. As you progress, learn, or even fail, you adjust. A plan that you create and don't *use* is pointless, so we'll share a few ways to turn your plan into a helpful guide. When you're done, you should feel capable, empowered, and excited to get started.

HOW TO CREATE A 90-DAY ACTION PLAN

In her late twenties, Marina took a big, big risk. She went to her boss and asked to take a remote year (this was long before *everybody* took a remote year). Through a program she had found, she would live in a different city around the world every month with a group of other professionals from different countries, industries, and backgrounds. Even though she felt she could make a strong case for how she could continue in her role and how it would benefit her and the company, she expected they wouldn't believe her team could perform without her in the office, and the answer would be no. She went for it anyway—and they said yes!

When we met Marina in our Fast Forward program, she was a few months away from leaving to embark on this "adventure." She was facing a year of uncertainty. Her job would change because she needed to shift away from her in-person management responsibilities. She would spend a year traveling with people she didn't know to places she had never been. She wasn't sure how her relationship with her boyfriend, Sean, would fare over a year of long-distance. She also recognized the potential pitfalls of what she was trying to accomplish—getting so busy with work that she couldn't enjoy the trip, getting so wrapped up in the travel that she checked out of her professional life, and getting so distracted by both that she wasn't connecting with Sean.

Because Marina was facing so much uncertainty, it was a perfect time for her to throw her hat over the wall, write a vision with bold, inspiring outcomes, and then develop an action plan to achieve it. The more uncertainty you're facing, the more important it is to be intentional, focused on controlling what you can, and clear about the outcomes that are most important to you. Marina chose three that would help her feel successful and take ground in her work, travel program, and relationship with Sean. Her vision included some less-than-concrete outcomes because of the nature of her work and the year ahead. If she didn't define specific actions, behaviors, and habits month after month, with a timeline for each, they could easily not happen.

The important takeaway from Marina's example (pages 134–135) is that our 90-Day Action Plan is not a "how to change everything in my life right now" plan. It's a few long-term outcomes, a few specific actions or habits that will help you make immediate progress toward those outcomes, and then a timeline for each. That's it. Simple. Remember, **it's not about doing more, it's about doing more of what's important**.

As you read on and learn how to create a plan that works for you, don't get hung up on creating the "perfect" plan. Create the plan that will help you make progress *now*. You can always course correct as you move forward. Ninety days is enough time to take action, make progress, and then *adjust*. Take a look at the series of actions Marina wrote for the outcome related to her travel program. She realized quickly that the program did a lot of things well but did not have a structure in place for professional development. If she wanted it, it would be up to her to create it. She decided the next action would be to survey others in her program to determine if they were interested in a monthly meeting. They were, so she added a new action to create a plan for the first session. She took it on soon after the program started, leading her fellow travelers through our bold vision exercise.

For many outcomes, your plan will require taking on new habits necessary for making progress on an outcome or to replace others that

Marina's 90-Day Action Plan Example

OUTCOME	ACTIONS/HABITS	TIMING
My team's work is stronger than ever. They are recognized across the organization for their stellar results and what they bring to the table. My leaders feel happy and proud that they sent me on this adventure.	In one-on-ones, dig deep into goals, skills development, and help needed with every person on my team.	Ongoing weekly starting the first week of July
	Gather feedback from cross-functional stakeholders on what the team needs to focus on most to improve performance.	By July 15
	Based on what I learn in one-on-ones, develop an outline for a training program for the two managers who report to me.	By August 1
	[Adjustment] Develop an outline for a modular training and development program that levels up the team's expertise and professionalism, based on what I learned about needs and goals.	By September 1

Sean and I feel connected and are communicating better than ever	We text with each other every day and speak on the phone or in video calls at least four times a week.	Starting September 1
	We see each other in person once every three months for a week.	Quarterly
	[Adjustment] Decide on timing of first visit and schedule travel.	By September 30
The travel abroad program is like a mini-MBA that is allowing me to network with and learn from people with diverse professional backgrounds and experience.	Identify the professional development opportunities that the program offers and assess which ones I'll try.	By September 1
	[Adjustment] Survey my cohort to assess their interest in a monthly workshop-like meeting where we share our expertise.	By September 30
	[Adjustment] Set a date, topic, and presenter for the first workshop.	By October 15

don't work or are reactive. Marina included communication habits in her plan because they would be necessary for her and Sean to feel connected across continents. You might include a habit to review your calendar for the coming week on Friday afternoons or plan meals for the week on Sundays. Research shows that on average, **most people need at least two months, and some need more, for a habit to become truly automatic.**[2] It depends on the person and on the difficulty of the habit you're trying to build. The 90-day approach should give you the time you need to cement a habit before shifting your energy and focus.

By the end of ninety days, you should feel proud of your progress, see the benefits in your life and work, and be ready to focus on a new habit or set of actions to keep you moving toward your vision for the next ninety days. Let's look at how to build your plan.

Step 1: Start with the Finish and Focus on the Few

Too often, when people finally decide to start planning, they create hyper-detailed plans for every aspect of their life, including things they're already doing and things they know how to accomplish. You don't need a plan for outcomes that are already happening. You only need a plan for outcomes from your vision that have these attributes:

- They are uncomfortable and unpredictable.
- You don't know how to accomplish them.
- You're relying on people and factors outside of your control.
- You could fail or have failed in the past.

The first step in our planning approach is identifying *no more than three* important outcomes from your vision that you want to start working on *now*. Start with the most uncomfortable or complicated or uncertain. Circle or highlight them in your vision. If you haven't created your vision yet, write outcomes that make the most sense for the life you want to be living now and in the future. We won't repeat how to write those outcomes (you can turn to chapter three for best practices), but we want to remind you that language creates reality, so they should be inspiring, clear, focused, and specific. Write them in a way that helps you know whether you're making progress, and be sure not to confuse an action with an outcome, like in the first example we've shared in the table.

Avoiding Pitfalls in Your Outcomes

Ineffective	Effective
Every week I'm having one-on-ones with my team. [An action, not an outcome]	My weekly one-on-ones leave people feeling empowered and in action.
I have better work-life balance. [Vague and impossible to know if you're succeeding]	I am placing importance on family time by having dinner with my family three nights a week and ending the workday by 6:30.
The team uses our time efficiently, and we're more productive. [Vague and impossible to know if you're succeeding]	We effectively manage our team's digital pipeline, resulting in 15 percent time savings per week.

Step 2: Identify the Next Specific Action You'll Take

How do you climb a mountain? One step at a time. That's what the actions and habits part of a plan should do for you. They keep you moving forward, step by step, without getting overwhelmed by all the things that might need to happen eventually. You don't need to map out everything you'll do over the next year or even the next ninety days. For some outcomes, you couldn't anyway because you don't yet know what those things will be. You need to be clear about what you will work on *today or this week*.

Your plan should include no more than three highly specific actions or habits for each outcome—any more than that and you'll become overwhelmed or distracted. When you accomplish those items, you can add more. When choosing and writing your actions or habits, be aware of a common pitfall. Sometimes, we think we're identifying a single step we want or need to take, but when we look at it as a prompt to take action, we realize it's actually many steps disguised as a single action. When we try to do it, we're overwhelmed and don't know where to begin. The key is to make each action a *single* thing to do. In the table, we've shown examples of the difference.

Avoiding Pitfalls in Your Actions or Habits

Ineffective	Effective
Start exercising. [overwhelming and vague]	Identify one yoga class at my gym that fits my schedule.
Develop our annual business plan. [too many steps, overwhelming]	Set up a meeting with my team to align on key business metrics for the year.
Stick to my monthly budget. [not clear how to do it or what to do]	Every Monday morning, write down how much I've spent so far for the month and how much I have left to spend before the end of the month.

Step 3: Commit to Timeline

As you saw in Marina's plan, **you need a "by when" date or a decision about frequency for each action or habit.** While your outcome may be bold and uncomfortable, you want your plan to be realistic in terms of timing. For instance, Marina's last day in the office would be September 4, so her in-person discussions and training with her direct reports had to be completed before then. Once she had finished that, she added new actions. Without a specific date to guide your focus, you *will* procrastinate or let other tasks or events push your plan to the side. Timelines are also helpful because they create a sense of progress and accomplishment that boosts your motivation and confidence.

We've shared outcome and action examples on pages 140–141 to give you some ideas or inspiration as you're creating your plan.

USE YOUR PLAN TO MAKE YOUR VISION A REALITY

Gabriel and Marina both tracked their lives, quarter by quarter, for a year. Doing so helped them achieve most of the outcomes in their visions. "I don't think I would have had such an enriching experience during my year abroad if I hadn't planned and been intentional," Marina said recently. The effects in her life were long-lasting. Her team was one of the highest-performing in the company because of the intensive training work she did, and because they were empowered to step up and tackle challenges in her absence. One of the unexpected outcomes of the year was that Marina realized how much she enjoyed training and development. It showed up in her actions with her team and with the people in her program. She now works with us at Fast Forward, an outcome that she put in her vision the following year! She still has monthly online professional development meetings with members of her travel group, and she and Sean are married and have a baby girl.

Marina's story highlights the fact that a plan, like a vision, isn't a static document that you create and then stick in a drawer. It's a dashboard for your whole life that helps you focus on how you're making your vision a reality, right now. Here are some tips for using your plan to help you remain intentional and maintain your inspiration and focus.

- **Keep it accessible.** Many people like to print their plan and put it on their desk, bulletin board, or bathroom mirror. Some people add it to their vision document. Some keep it on their laptop or phone. Do what works for you!
- **Review it weekly.** Are you devoting time, energy, and focus to the actions and habits that will help you make progress? Where do

90-Day Action Plan Examples

OUTCOME	ACTIONS/HABITS	TIMING
I am in control of my calendar and have six hours weekly to think and strategically plan.	Weekly meeting audit.	Start July 1
	Insert daily "no interruption" time into my day and stick to it.	July 15
	Request agenda for every meeting to determine my role.	Start July 15
We are delivering Fast Forward virtual workshop series to ten existing clients, and four new clients enabling us to keep annual revenue flat during the pandemic.	Deliver virtual workshop series with two clients; gather their feedback and improve.	July 30
	Share new product with twenty existing clients to generate demand and get referrals.	July 30
	Develop prospect list for companies focused on engagement, retention, and team building.	August 30

We have a culture where people feel appreciated and safe to try new things and innovate.	Recommend that in every team meeting, we acknowledge two	July 1
	Share my vision with my team.	July 15
	Ask my team for ideas on other ways to champion a culture where we root for each other's success.	Start July 1, check in monthly
I am confidently communicating my point of view, regardless of the audience or group.	Make one recommendation to accelerate business each week.	Start July 1 (ongoing)
	Share my aspiration with my manager and ask for support.	July 15
	Register for internal public speaking workshop.	By July 15
I feel energetic and look amazing. I live healthily every day and have lost ten pounds. I am proud.	Download Headspace app and try it one time.	July 1
	Exercise at least three times a week for minimum of thirty minutes.	Start July 15
	Schedule meeting with nutritionist.	July 30

you need to adjust? What new actions or habits should you add based on what you've accomplished or learned? (You might only do this monthly so that you don't become overwhelmed.) Track your progress and setbacks and celebrate your wins.

- **Share it.** A plan is a great tool for asking others for ideas or to hold you accountable. As you did with your vision, share it with your buddy, your partner, your boss, your team. Share the parts you are comfortable sharing with the people who can help the most.

- **Update it quarterly.** Every ninety days, update the outcomes you're working on. You might change some of them or none of them, depending on the progress you've made or the complexity of the outcome.

When You Fail (and You Will), Reset

When Lisa's daughter, Caroline, was being recruited for highly ranked college lacrosse programs, Lisa met with many coaches. She's deeply curious about what it takes to be a high performer, so she would ask each coach, "Given the thousands of women competing for the eight spots on your team, what attributes do you look for?" The response was always the same: The most successful athletes are those who can press the reset button between plays, quarters, and games. Serena Williams echoed this sentiment in an interview, sharing that a key to her success is her ability to reset between each point, especially those that don't go her way, so that she can focus on what she has to do to win the *next* point.

The ability to accept when things don't go as planned—a lost deal, critical feedback, not getting a promotion, other people not delivering, or not following through on a new habit—is an absolutely critical skill for anybody pushing toward a bold vision. A setback today does not mean a setback forever, or even tomorrow. So when you don't fulfill your plan or achieve an outcome in a certain period of time, practice resetting.

For some people, resetting is as simple as taking a deep clearing breath. For others, it might involve clearing a power outage, especially if their inner critic is ranting away. It might even require taking a step back and looking at what limiting beliefs or stories are in play so that you can choose a more empowering perspective. Find what works best for you in different situations—and then practice.

Planning creates time and space to address the challenges you're facing and determine at least a few things you could do to achieve your most important outcomes, even if you don't know everything you'll need to do. It allows you to start making progress now rather than later. As you achieve small goals, you feel capable and confident, which makes it more likely that you'll achieve small goals, feeding your motivation and productivity.

In the next chapter, we'll help you tackle the most common impediment to turning your plans into those small wins—saying yes to things that don't align with your vision or plan. If you'd like to feel comfortable and confident saying no, read on.

Chapter 10

SAYING NO
WITHOUT GUILT

J eff wanted to be liked. Don't we all? He is a genuinely nice, helpful guy, but that helpful nature had morphed into an automatic response to say yes to almost any call for help. Whether the question was "Can I pick your brain about this issue?" or "Can you attend this meeting and share your perspective?" or "Could you review this slide deck?" his answer was almost always yes. People turned to him for help so often partially because he had been with his company for almost ten years. He was a fount of institutional knowledge and had done every job in his department. He was their short-cut. "Even if I had six things I needed to knockout in a day," he said, "suddenly that other person's needs were priority number one."

Jeff's Fast Forward coach asked him to track how many meetings or assists he said yes to for a week. At the end, he discovered it was *a lot*. "When you're in that mindset of *I need to say yes*, you usually believe that you're high performing," he told us. "When you're wearing seven hats, you're thinking, *I'm impressing my bosses*, when in fact, you're probably just doing average work across the board. You're working incredibly hard to produce that average work, though." Volumes and volumes of research on how distractions affect the quality of our work and thinking supports Jeff's observation.

It was obvious that if Jeff wanted to be good at his job, get some exercise in, have a nice dinner with his wife, and maybe even get a good night's sleep—all aspects of his vision and plan—he would have to build his comfort and confidence in saying no. His first step was to be more rigorous about asking important questions: Is this mission critical? Do people really need my help? Am I doing my actual job right now? Then he began practicing the strategies we'll share for saying no effectively and without fear.

Within a month, this practice made a monumental difference in his life and for the members of his team, who were more empowered. When he and his coach caught up and she asked what was different, he said, "I have all this time on my hands now." That was uncomfortable, too, but he soon found ways to use it to level up his most important work. To this day, he's still well-liked, still considered a helpful and supportive leader and colleague, and even more of a rock star in the company.

If you can relate to Jeff's story, you're not alone. Saying yes when we shouldn't or don't want to is a reactive, unconscious behavior that's so pervasive it stands in a class all its own. It's a huge obstacle to achieving our plans and visions and creating the life we want. Overcoming it requires us to say no to our own reactive behavior *and say no to other people*.

Sometimes we say yes because it's something we've always said yes to in the past and we're operating on autopilot. Sometimes we say yes to avoid doing something uncomfortable or risky. For example, "I *had* to help Alice with her slides so I couldn't have that coaching conversation with Simon." Often, though, we're simply uncomfortable saying no to others. Like Jeff, we want people to like us, we feel guilty, or we fear the consequences. We're afraid that people might judge us, that our reputation will take a hit, or that we'll be seen as "not a team player." We don't want to let people down, especially people *we've conditioned* to expect a "yes." "Saying no is bad" is a limiting belief with high costs. We give away our power and control over our time and focus.

We also overlook or don't place enough value on the pure joy of *not* doing something so that we *can* do something else more essential to our success and happiness. One of our mantras at Fast Forward is "**move from FOMO to JOMO**"—**from the fear of missing out to the joy of missing out.** Regularly, we see people discover the joy of saying, "I don't need to be included in every meeting" or "I don't have to be involved in solving that challenge" or "I'm delighted to *not* go to that dinner so that I can stay home and relax."

In *The Power of a Positive No*, William Ury (more famous for coauthoring the classic on negotiation *Getting to Yes*), writes, "When we know how to use it correctly, this one word has the power to profoundly transform our lives for the better."[1] Saying no is one of the most critical and empowering skills you can develop. You can train yourself to get past the discomfort by using simple strategies that make saying no a normal part of your day. In this chapter, we'll help you

- Explore where in life you're saying yes without asking critical questions, like "Does this serve me?" and "What is the cost?"
- Create a personalized "Say No" list.
- Develop an effective approach and diplomatic language for saying no in all kinds of circumstances.

Our intention is to help you become more confident and comfortable saying no so you can spend more time saying yes to the things that light you up, propel you forward in meaningful ways, and leave you feeling fulfilled and proud.

MAKE YOUR CHOICE INTENTIONAL

You can take advantage of the power of no by being more aware and rigorous. Every time you say yes or no, it should be an *intentional choice you're making*.

Begin by looking at stories you're telling yourself about what's within your control and what isn't, or where you need to spend your time and where you don't, or what's possible to change and what isn't. Disempowering stories in these areas can make us reactive to requests. Jeff is a perfect example. He had been telling himself a story for years that he couldn't say no if he wanted to be liked or respected, but he obviously could.

Remind yourself that **you don't *have* to do anything**. When your client asks you to take a call on the weekend and you say yes, that's *your* choice. When somebody asks you to volunteer for a project or an event and you say yes, that's *your* choice. Shifting to this empowering perspective can give you clarity and open up possibilities.

Next, **let your higher commitment guide you.** One of our program participants was a single mom. After years spent saying yes to meetings that kept her at work until six or seven o'clock and feeling guilty, she decided to leave at four o'clock every day to meet her son at the bus, help him with homework, and have dinner together. Saying no to meeting requests after four o'clock became easy over time because she was vividly clear about her yes—making sure her son had somebody to be with in the evenings. As William Ury describes it, "Perhaps the single biggest mistake we make when we say No is to start from No. We derive our No from what we are against—the other's demand or behavior . . . Instead of starting from No, start from Yes. Root your No in a deeper Yes—a Yes to your core interests and to what truly matters."[2] This is the power of having a vision and a 90-Day Action Plan—they clarify your higher-level commitment to a future different from the past and to the things that are most important to you.

Before you say no too quickly, though, consider this: **You don't have to like it.** By that, we mean, you don't have to like everything you do and sometimes you definitely won't like some of the things you have to do to achieve your vision. Saying no to everything you don't like doing is just as reactive as saying yes when it doesn't serve you. Countless leaders in our programs have talked about how much they "dread" performance reviews. They also know how important it is to make sure they have the right talent in place, help people learn and grow, and discuss career development plans. They do the reviews and appreciate the results. When you feel you need to say yes to something you don't like, try to adjust your language to reflect a more empowered mindset. For instance, instead of saying, "Ugh, I've got to get to the gym tonight," say, "I'm looking forward to how going to the gym tonight will make me feel" or "I *get* to go to the gym tonight." If there's something you *have* to do to achieve a goal, find the *choice* you're making and embrace it.

CREATE A "SAY NO" LIST

Wendy: When I was making the choice to move away from my comfortable, solo executive coaching practice to make a bigger impact and to pursue greater career potential (the story Lisa shared in chapter one), I had a general idea of what I wanted to do next, but I needed concentrated periods of time to research, to think, to strategize, and to talk with other people in my industry. With three kids, an almost full-time job, and a husband with his own high-pressure career, that time wasn't going to magically appear. I needed to clear the field, so I did something that was incredibly scary: I decided to say no to new clients. Next, I stopped renewing clients I had coached for years. Gary said, "You're turning down all this work. What's your plan?" I said, "I don't know, but I'll never figure it out if I'm busy all the time."

By intentionally giving myself this space and time, I was open to discussing possibilities with Lisa when she was at a critical crossroads. Together, we launched The Fast Forward Group. Without those key nos it may never have happened.

When Lisa and I began building The Fast Forward Group, which would require intense bouts of work and a lot of travel, I had to get even more granular and rigorous about when I would say yes or no. One of my first steps was to create a "say no" list: I won't agree to be the room parent. I won't schedule more than two social plans a week. I won't say yes to work that doesn't align with our business development strategy. I did what it took to remove things from my life that I deemed less important, and I asked for or found help to get the necessities done. Making these choices *in advance* helped me safeguard my time so that I was doing the most important things to me, my family, and my business. One year, I said no to being the class parent, but I flew across the globe from Hong Kong after a three-day workshop to get back home in time to see my daughter perform in a play—because that was important to us both.

Saying no is easier when you're prepared. Getting clear about what you *won't* do because it isn't a priority or because it would force you to say no to your own priorities is a great way to deal with the discomfort in advance rather than in the moment, when you're more likely to be reactive. Requests that might come up in the short or long term, like the following, are a good place to start.

- Work on the weekend
- Take on a new project or client beyond your reasonable workload
- Help a colleague with a time-consuming project
- Go to a social event when you need time to relax or exercise
- Do a time-consuming favor for a friend
- Do other people's work while they are on vacation or leave
- Give younger professionals thirty minutes of your time to network

Where could you say no without a negative consequence—and with a positive one? When you ask yourself this question and answer it as objectively as possible, you'll find many opportunities. You'll discover that you're investing time and energy in things that don't align with your vision or the life you're trying to create. The following exercise, with reflection questions, will take you deeper and guide you to create your own personalized "say no" list. Give yourself the gift of preparation.

EXERCISE: CREATE A "SAY NO" LIST

1. Look at your calendar for the last few weeks. What are some things you said yes to and regretted, resented, or paid a price for doing? What are you currently saying yes to regularly that doesn't line up with your priorities and vision or that you just don't care about?
2. Look at your calendar for the next two to three weeks *and* the commitments you've made in your 90-Day Action Plan. What kinds of requests might you get that will require you to say no to a person or people if you want to meet those commitments?

HOW TO SAY NO

With clarity on where you *could* say no to behaviors or commitments that are sabotaging your time or energy, you can now work on building confidence in your ability to *do it*. The best way to begin is with a process and language that you can apply in all kinds of circumstances. That's what we'll share in the rest of this chapter.

Step 1: Acknowledge and validate the request. For instance, "It sounds like you have a really tight deadline and need additional support to get this project done."

Step 2 (Optional): Gather more intel.

- **Ask for more information to help you make an intentional decision.** Often, people ask somebody to get involved before they've assessed the role they want the person to play or whether they even need help. You might ask, "What's your timeline?" or "What role do you envision me playing?" People can be just as reactive in making requests as they can be in saying yes to requests.

- **Ask for time to consider the request.** You don't have to respond right away. You can take time to determine if it's something you can say yes to without sacrificing your plan and priorities. For instance, "Let me get back to you on this tomorrow. I need to look at my schedule and figure out if it's realistic."

Step 3: Say no, clearly and succinctly. Have you ever said something like, "Maybe I could squeeze it in, but I have so much on my plate right now. I'm not sure it would be a good idea to take it on. I have this new project . . . " What's the other person supposed to take away from that? Be straightforward and firm. Once you've said no, stop talking. Don't give a long explanation. You may think the other person cares why you're saying no, but they don't. Don't bury the no in caveats or say, "I don't think" or "If only . . . " It leaves the other person unsure, and they're likely to come back to you again. Give them and yourself the respect of being clear. For instance, "Given what's on my plate, I can't help you with that project right now."

Remember: "No" is a complete sentence.

That said, **sometimes being transparent about why we're saying no gives us an opportunity to share elements of our vision or plan or remind people of shared commitments.** For instance, if a friend invites you to go to happy hour but you're working on a habit of getting to the gym after work, say so. "I'd love to see you. I'm also committed to getting healthier this year and this is supposed to be a gym day for me." Sometimes there's a shared commitment to raise, especially in the workplace. "As a team we've made a commitment that senior leaders won't attend project planning meetings unless there's a major challenge to solve. That doesn't sound like the case here."

Step 4 (If applicable): Make a counteroffer. Recommend or request an alternative solution, activity, or timeline. For instance, "If you still need help in two weeks, I could lend a hand then" or "I know somebody who would appreciate the opportunity to be involved. Could I connect you?" or "I'm working on building healthier habits. Why don't we go for a walk instead of happy hour?"

Now it's your turn. You'll feel more confident saying no if you develop your own language for the kinds of requests you get most often. We've shared many examples for inspiration in the following list. Even three or four key phrases could make a difference and help you work through the discomfort. Once you have them, post them where they're easily accessible when you need them. Stick them on your wall, in a note on your phone, or on your desktop—and use them often!

EXAMPLES OF HOW TO SAY NO

- Oh, I will be so disappointed to miss this! Thank you for asking me.
- I'm not available, but I know someone who would love to be a part of it. May I connect you?
- I am so flattered that you asked, but unfortunately I need to decline. I do hope you'll keep me in mind for the future.
- I can't attend that meeting, but I could help by sending you [an in-depth video tutorial on how this product works; a resource we just developed for marketing; a few

recent articles that I found insightful; a transcript of a recent client call].

- I sit down with my calendar on Sundays. Would you please send me all of the information and I'll let you know on Monday if it works with my schedule?
- Thank you for reaching out to me. I'm booked solid for the next [X weeks or months]. If we could begin on [X date], it's worth us having a deeper conversation about the project.
- I know you asked me because you thought [I'd enjoy it, it would be a good fit for me, I'd appreciate the opportunity]. This isn't the kind of [project/work/volunteering] I usually take on.

Imagine you took everything you learned in this chapter and put it into action tomorrow. What difference would that make in your life, if you started saying no to other people and to your own reactivity? Would it reduce your stress and resentment? Increase your peace and joy? "Create" time for rewarding and exciting work? Help you achieve greater success because you can focus on mission critical activities?

That's what we want for you. In the next Power Principle, we're going to keep up the focus on effective communication so you can enroll people in your vision and help them take action.

Power Principle 4

USE LANGUAGE OF ACTION

*Get Out of the Stands
and Onto the Field*

Chapter 11

COMMUNICATE WITH INTENTION— AND PROPEL THINGS FORWARD

B rad was in the middle of a career transition. His company had been purchased by another, and in the reshuffle, he had been laid off. He had the right perspective, though—looking at it as an opportunity to shift away from one line of work and into another that he found more interesting and exciting. Over his fifteen years in his industry, he had developed an incredible network. "Start there," Wendy suggested during a coaching call. "Create a spreadsheet of all the people who could potentially help you find the kind of role you want."

Once Brad had his list, Wendy suggested he write down what he would ask of each person, such as an introduction or a lead on opportunities. He committed to reaching out to a few people in his network every week.

A few weeks later, she asked him how it was going? "Terribly," he said. "Nothing's happening." That wasn't the outcome they had intended, obviously, so Wendy dug in. "Did you reach out?" Yes, he'd had calls and lunches. "Were they receptive and friendly?" Yes, they were. "Describe a specific conversation you had this week, from beginning to end." As he did, she immediately saw the problem: *he had never made a specific request.* He told them what he was trying to accomplish, but he never said, "Would you be willing to introduce me to X" or "Would you let me know of any opportunities at Y." People were probably completely unaware that Brad was *hoping for* their support. (And remember, hope is not a strategy.)

Brad's experience might feel familiar. In the last few months, you likely had an important conversation with an outcome that was *far* from what you wanted it to be. Maybe you left a meeting and thought, *That's an hour of my life I'll never get back.* Or if you're like most people, you had a conversation with your partner or kids to try to shift household habits . . . and nothing changed. These moments of frustration happen to all of us—because too often, we're *ineffective* communicators.

The problem is universal. In one study of more than five hundred companies around the globe, people said that they spend more than *seventeen hours* every week addressing the fallout of poor, unclear communication—waiting for information, being bombarded with irrelevant information, trying to get teams aligned on the same information.[1] And in our personal lives, the problem is just as widespread. According to *many* surveys, therapists believe that communication problems are the number one cause of relationship breakdowns in marriages, families, and friend groups.

Even people who are effective in some situations, like inspiring a team, are ineffective in others, like asking a client to sign a new contract. Brad's story is a perfect explanation. Like most of us, he was completely unaware that he *wasn't* being clear, and he was uncomfortable being direct. When Wendy asked him what he thought was getting in the way, he said, "I don't want to seem pushy or needy. They're all really busy. I don't want to put something else on their plate." His unconscious communication habits and his discomfort were keeping him from achieving his goals.

>>

**How you communicate will either accelerate or impede
your progress toward the results, and the life, you want.**

>>

Most of your big goals will require the support and involvement of other people. Being intentional and **using *language of action* will help you confidently and effectively influence what they think, what they choose to do, and how motivated they are to make it happen**—whether it's getting a new client to green-light a proposal, getting your team to deliver on a deadline, or getting your partner to help you stick to a budget. You'll share ideas and recommendations with conviction and leave people clear and inspired.

In this Power Principle, we'll give you the clarity and tools to make clear communication happen. We'll begin in this chapter by helping you understand the difference between being in the stands, using language of observation, and being on the field, using language of action. We'll help you understand what's keeping you from getting on the field and where doing so could make a difference in your life. And we'll go deep on how to break away from the most disempowering form of in-the-stands communication—complaining.

WHAT IS LANGUAGE OF ACTION?

The best way to understand what we mean by the phrase "language of action" is to imagine that you're at a football game and you're sitting in the stands. What kinds of things would you be saying? You might be analyzing the odds, predicting the outcome, cheering for the players, complaining about the ref, or educating the person next to you—whether they want you to or not. While there is value in this type of language, does any of it move the ball down the field?

Now imagine that you're on the field, as a coach or player. What kinds of things would you be saying? You'd be determining the desired outcome for the next play. You'd be coordinating with other players or directing them on what to do and when. You'd be motivating them to get the intended result. You would use **language that helped move the ball down the field.**

Two Forms of Communication

In the Stands, Using Language of Observation	On the Field, Using Language of Action

• Praising
• Analyzing
• Describing
• Predicting or forecasting
• Educating or informing
• Complaining
	• Setting a desired outcome
	• Making recommendations and requests
	   ○ Taking a stand
	   ○ Asking for help
	   ○ Aligning on *who* is doing *what* by *when*

Language of action is direct, specific, and compelling. It brings people on board with your vision and plan.

In our daily lives, and especially in the workplace, we spend a lot of time in the stands, educating, informing, describing, analyzing, or praising. Being in the stands can be valuable, *when that's where we should be and when we're intentional about being there.* **Too often, we're in the stands when we should be on the field.** We're *un*intentionally and *un*consciously in the stands. Like Brad, we might even think we *are* on the field—but we aren't. Then, we're frustrated because nothing happens, nothing changes, and we're left spinning our wheels. It happens in all parts of our lives, and we may not realize the cost until it's too late. Let's look at what keeps us from getting on the field so that we don't keep experiencing that cost.

WHAT'S KEEPING YOU FROM GETTING ON THE FIELD

We worked with a woman in sales, Chelsea, who had an aha moment during one of our communication workshops. "We think we're selling," she said, "but all we're doing is educating and informing clients about our products. We're in the stands." She was right. Their presentation had fifteen generic slides about their products before they got around to discussing how they could help the client. Even when they did, they often weren't making a specific request or recommendation for how to move forward. Their clients often took no action after these meetings. As a team, they had been barely hitting their sales targets. And until that moment, they didn't realize how they were communicating or the impact it was having.

With everything we know about the costs of *ineffective* communication —the wasted time and resources, the breakdown in relationships, the hit to collaboration and innovation—why aren't we better at it? Many of us haven't been taught how to be effective, and as we've said, often we're simply unconscious and unintentional. Even people whose job depends on using language of action often may not be *consistently* good at it. Why?

Staying in the stands feels comfortable and safe. Being on the field, using language of action, means advocating for our ideas, asking for help or support, and building buy-in—and that all feels risky. You can reread the brain science we shared in chapter two about our aversion to risk, but when it comes to getting on the field, here are some of our common mental hurdles.

- We don't want to seem like we are pushing too hard or coming on too strong.
- We're afraid of going out on a limb and challenging the status quo. We worry about the potential backlash.
- We don't want to be judged if the action we're encouraging doesn't work out.
- We're afraid the answer might be "no."

- We don't want to seem incapable if we ask for help (especially because some of us have limiting beliefs in that area).

In *Crucial Conversations*, the author team, who are social scientists, describes the outcome of all this angst: "When conversations matter the most—that is, when conversations move from casual to crucial—we're generally on our worst behavior."[2] When we are stressed, anxious, or sense conflict, our executive functioning and higher-order reasoning take a hit. The result is that *what* we communicate and *how* are often "perfectly designed to keep us from what we actually want."

How do you get past your discomfort—conscious or unconscious? By being intentional.

Being Intentional Is How You Become Effective

In the last Power Principle, we said that being intentional, rather than reactive, with your time, energy, and focus is how you make progress on your vision. The same is true with communication.

The best strategy for getting on the field and communicating in a way that forwards action is to be intentional.

What do we mean by that? Be intentional in getting clear about the outcomes you're trying to achieve. Be intentional in how you'll achieve those outcomes by *preparing* to make them happen. Too often, we don't do either, or we don't go far enough. **We have good intentions, but we go into conversations and meetings unprepared to deliver on them.** We feel too busy to prepare so we end up winging it and hoping for the best. When we're in the moment, we end up letting our discomfort rule us and avoid things that should be said or that could make the biggest impact, like

Brad did. Then, we leave without clarity, and nothing moves forward. We don't make progress on our goals or vision.

In the next two chapters, we'll give you models and tools for making sure that rarely happens to you. They're the same tools Chelsea and her team used—once they recognized they were stuck in the stands and the cost of being there. Almost immediately, they saw improvements in meeting effectiveness, client relationships, and numbers of closed deals.

You can see the same kind of immediate results in your life. First, you have to identify where you should be on the field to begin with.

WHERE SHOULD YOU BE ON THE FIELD?

Lisa: I love being on the field. I make a lot of requests and recommendations. More than half of the time I don't get a yes, especially from my husband. He even found a strategic loophole: "Maybe." He says it so often, he bought a big red button he could push that says it for him. In order to stay married, I had to stop myself from throwing it out the back door.

The people in my life can find the flow of recommendations and requests that come from me annoying (even Wendy can feel overwhelmed sometimes), but I temper it by being okay with getting a "no." I see it as a numbers game. Even if I get a yes only 30 percent of the time, I'm making a lot of things happen. It helps that I often relate to a "no" as a "yes" waiting to happen.

Back when I was leading large corporate teams and had an office, I posted a sign over my door: "Requests and Recommendations Welcome." This let people know that I wanted them on the field, using language of action. I wanted them to come to me with solutions. Being on the field has been key to achieving outcomes from my own vision *and* creating a healthy culture of goal achievement with the teams I've led.

An amazing thing happens when you ask for what you want—you often get it. You can't force people to comply, but you can enroll them in your vision by using language of action. You won't always get a yes, but as Lisa said, if you keep suggesting, keep advocating, and keep taking a stand, you *will* make progress. To help kickstart your thinking, here are some common examples of places people get on the field to achieve their visions.

- Asking for a promotion or a raise
- Reducing time spent in meetings
- Asking a person or team to take on more responsibility
- Improving a relationship
- Developing flexible work arrangements
- Reducing weekend work or email
- Improving the company culture
- Advocating for better benefits
- Sharing household or caregiver responsibilities

Now it's your turn. Use this exercise to identify an area of your life where you could be on the field—and the difference it would make.

EXERCISE: GETTING ON THE FIELD

- Where in your life would it make a difference to get out of the stands and onto the field? (Look for clues in areas of your life where you're complaining a lot or where you feel frustrated, stuck, stressed out, unseen, or unheard — or you're just not making progress.)
- What's getting in the way?
- What's the cost?
- What difference would it make to you and others if you got on the field?

THE HIGH COST OF COMPLAINING

Every week, Alex had to attend a meeting with the management team. It was on Thursday afternoons at 4:30, and almost always ran longer than the ninety minutes scheduled. Calling in was frowned upon. He had to spend at least two hours the day before preparing for it—reading reports, getting updates on key projects, anticipating questions that would come up. He felt it was a waste of time for him and the whole leadership team because not much changed from week to week. The late start and long run time also meant he often missed family commitments or social events. This one meeting made him feel resentful and even angry. For a year, he complained about it at work and at home—and for a year, he didn't do one thing about it. He just complained and felt resigned. "I carried a low-grade annoyance in the background all of the time," he told us. It affected his feelings about his work and his boss and made him grumpy at home on the days around the meeting.

>>

One of the biggest complaints in companies, families, and friend groups is that everyone is complaining, all the time!

>>

And yet, we don't even realize how often we do it. Consider this question. How much time do you spend complaining *every week* . . . out loud . . . at work? An hour? Two hours? More? *Probably*. Author and leadership expert Marshall Goldsmith reviewed a survey that found that most employees spend at least ten hours a month, or about two and a half hours a week, complaining or listening to others complain *just about leaders in their companies*. He didn't believe it, so he surveyed two hundred of his own clients—and got the same results.[3] Those were the hours spent complaining *about bosses out loud*. What about silent or internal complaints? What about the time spent complaining about other teams, colleagues, the service we get, our families, politics, financial struggles, and on and on? When we ask people, the majority say that they spend at least 30 percent of their waking hours complaining, and we're sure they're underestimating.

–––––––––––––––––––––––– >> ––––––––––––––––––––––––

Imagine how much time and emotional energy you would get back if you could break the complaint cycle.

–––––––––––––––––––––––– >> ––––––––––––––––––––––––

The costs are enormous. When we complain often, day after day, about even minor frustrations, we can end up feeling "helpless, victimized, and bad about ourselves," explains psychologist Guy Winch, author of *The Squeaky Wheel*.[4] Complaining usually falls into two categories: complaining about things *outside of* our control and complaining about things *within* our control. Complaining about things *outside* of our control reinforces the sense that we can't change things for the better. Over time, it affects our outlook, mindset, and motivation. If you're complaining regularly about something out of your control (like the length of your commute), we recommend trying to choose a new perspective so that you're investing less energy in something that's unchangeable.

Complaining about things *within our power* to change or improve keeps us in the stands, like Alex, and holds us back from our visions. **Imagine how different things could be if you got on the field and turned your complaints into recommendations or requests.** We've said that in-the-stands communication can be valuable. Occasionally, complaining offers benefits. When we complain with others, it creates a sense of bonding, and complaints can be a source of ideas or innovation (think about how many product improvements have come from customer complaints). Of course, that means seeing the opportunity, need, or commitment behind the complaint—*because if we didn't care, we wouldn't complain.*

When you're ready to get out of the stands and break *your* complaint cycle, start with this exercise.

EXERCISE: TURNING COMPLAINTS INTO REQUESTS OR RECOMMENDATIONS

Identify a complaint you've had for some time about something you can control or at least influence.

1. What's the commitment behind the complaint?
   Example: Alex's commitment was to improve the quality and impact of the meeting, to give everyone back a few hours of time, and to be able to meet his personal commitments on those days.

2. How would you like it to look?
   Alex wanted the meeting to be less frequent, more efficient, and to start and end earlier.

Considering these questions helped Alex realize that he wasn't powerless to change the situation. He approached his manager and made several recommendations to make the meeting more efficient and require less prep time for everybody. He also recommended meeting biweekly instead of weekly and starting an hour earlier. Alex made a strong case, and his boss agreed. Within a few weeks, Alex felt less frustrated and more in control of his time. "I will never again spend a year complaining about something I could change," he said.

When you turn your in-the-stands complaints into on-the-field recommendations and requests, you will reclaim your power to create the life you want.

Feeling uncomfortable being direct with people is part of being human. Being unaware that we aren't being clear or effective is too. It's how we're wired, but that doesn't mean we're stuck with our communication habits or that we're powerless to improve. The rest of this Power Principle offers tools that will make you a confident, *effective* communicator. Using them will help you transform conversations and meetings into opportunities to build relationships, produce results, and make progress on your vision and plans.

Chapter 12

DO YOU KNOW YOUR DESIRED OUTCOME?

Carrie had been conducting the same annual meeting with one of her company's largest clients for three years. "It's the usual dog and pony show," she told us about a week before the next one. We were in a session with her team discussing making meetings productive. "Our top people meet their top people. We show them our new capabilities. We have lunch. We do a tour. At the end of the day, we shake hands and everybody flies home."

"You don't seem especially excited about such a high-level meeting," Wendy said.

"I honestly don't know what we get out of it, and it takes up a lot of time for a lot of people. I guess we're building the relationship, but it's hard to pinpoint any specific results."

It was a classic in-the-stands meeting. Maybe you can relate. They were educating and informing, not driving action to move the business forward. There's nothing wrong with relationship building, but Carrie had an opportunity to make this meeting about so much more. Lisa jumped in. "Carrie, let's start with the finish. This is a meeting with one of your company's largest accounts. You're inviting leaders from both sides to spend a full day together. Fast-forward to the end of the meeting. What do you want them to believe, feel, and as a result, do next?"

Carrie thought about the question for a moment. "I want them to leave the meeting feeling that we have a genuine commitment to helping them achieve *their* business goals. I want them to believe that our products are uniquely positioned to grow their customer base. And I want them to share this conviction with their teams. *That* would have a ripple effect throughout their company and ours. Their teams would trust us more. Our work together would be more efficient. That would make this day worth the time and money we spend on it."

"What would you do differently to make that happen?" she asked. Carrie thought for a moment and smiled, "Instead of doing the usual product capability overview, we'd spend the day showing them how our products can help them reach their specific customer base. It could be really engaging and interactive." Carrie was now genuinely excited—and she realized the team had to change the agenda given the desired outcome. She was ready to get on the field.

Carrie emailed us the day after the meeting. "Yesterday was a huge success. I kicked off the meeting by sharing my desired outcome. It felt risky, but it changed the energy and the trajectory of the day. Our conversations were engaging and interactive because they were focused on their needs and interests versus our products. The most exciting part is that I'm confident this meeting will transform our partnership over the coming year, not only for the people in the meeting but also for the teams that work on this account. We'll never approach these high-level meetings the same way again."

When was the last time you were in a meeting or conversation where the person started with such intention, as Carrie did? Most people and teams don't prepare or communicate in this way, and meetings suffer because of it. Three experts from Harvard Business School and Boston University surveyed 182 senior managers about meetings: 71 percent said they're unproductive and inefficient, and "62% said meetings miss opportunities to bring the team closer together."[1] They don't produce alignment, effective collaboration, or better execution—because people aren't intentional about why they're meeting or what result they're working toward. (No wonder management guru Patrick Lencioni wrote a book titled *Death by Meeting*!)

You can make every conversation and meeting more effective and productive by choosing to be *intentional*.

>>

The first step is to set a desired outcome. Ask yourself, "At the end of this conversation, what will they believe, how will they feel, and as a result, what will they do?"

>>

This may sound simple, but it requires a lot of practice. First, you have to start with the finish. Notice that the question begins with "At the end of this conversation." As with writing your vision, you have to imagine yourself and your audience in the future, feeling satisfied with the conversation or meeting.

Second, you have to consider your audience's perspective. We can't tell you how many times we've heard someone say, "My desired outcome is that management approves my budget request" or "My desired outcome is that my in-laws stay at a hotel when they visit." Nope. Neither of those reflects what the audience cares about. If you don't begin by considering their perspective, you can't influence what they believe, feel, or do. You'll have a hard time motivating them to take a specific action as the conversation progresses. This is how you **build a connection between what you each want and need** and *avoid* coming across as self-serving or pushing your own agenda.

Our participants say that setting a desired outcome is one of the most transformative practices they learn in our program. Many clients have used it to change their entire meeting culture. When somebody sends out a meeting invite, they're required to include the desired outcome. Can you imagine the difference that would make for you, knowing why you're there and how best to contribute to achieve the desired outcome? How much time would you save? We hear over and over from our graduates that their meetings are shorter, they stay on track, and they produce the intended outcome—rather than producing the need for *another* meeting. In their personal lives, setting desired outcomes has helped them have effective conversations about starting a family, tackling financial challenges, sharing household responsibilities, resolving family and friend group dysfunction, and more.

In this chapter, we'll share prescriptive coaching to help you achieve the same kind of results in your life. By the end, you will feel ready to set desired outcomes with confidence and conviction. Then, in the next chapter, we'll give you the tools to prepare for the rest of the conversation so that you can make sure that outcome happens! Every time you do this, you'll be taking a small step toward the goals you're trying to achieve.

SETTING A DESIRED OUTCOME

1. Who is your audience and what do they care about?
2. At the end of the conversation, what will they believe, feel, and do?
3. How will your audience benefit?

1. WHO IS YOUR AUDIENCE AND WHAT DO THEY CARE ABOUT?

To give somebody a reason to care about what you have to say, you need to stand in their shoes. Without deep insight into your audience, you might as well be talking to yourself. Carrie knew her clients well and understood their challenges and goals, what felt hard, and what hurdles they were facing. That isn't always the case.

Frank was on the sustainability committee at a large financial services company when we met him in a Fast Forward program. He was passionate about the environment and dedicated hours to this work in addition to his demanding day job. "I'm meeting with Jackie, the CFO, to make the annual ask for resources for sustainability projects in the coming year," he told us when we asked if anybody had an important meeting coming up. Then, with resignation: "We never get what we ask for." Heading into an important meeting resigned to it not going your way *is not* a quick path to success, so we dove into the first question to try to shift his thinking.

"Frank, what does Jackie care about?" As simple as this question is, Frank hadn't given it much thought. He knew what request he wanted to make and the rationale, but he honestly had no idea what Jackie cared about.

"Protecting the budget?" he said.

"Yes, but we're sure she cares about more than that, like supporting the success of the company." Frank began to see there could be value in finding out what that was. After our meeting, he did some homework. He almost couldn't believe it when he discovered that Jackie was on the board of a nonprofit dedicated to water conservation. She was also new to the firm and had yet to take on anything outside of her day-to-day role. Frank's perspective on the meeting began to shift.

If you don't know what your audience cares about, take the time to find out. Ask questions. Do research. And check your assumptions. What most business leaders care about is accelerating revenue, driving growth, improving operations, reducing costs, or improving delivery timelines. However, they're also human beings who care about things like making contributions that help them get promoted, feeling proud of the work they're doing, and—let's be honest—keeping their jobs. Don't forget to consider the whole picture, like Frank did.

2. AT THE END OF THE CONVERSATION, WHAT WILL PEOPLE BELIEVE, FEEL, AND DO?

This is worth repeating: If you can influence what people believe and how they feel, they're more likely to agree with or follow through on your recommendation or request. Consider this question carefully. What impact do you want to have on people's mindset? What does success look like at the end? Let's say somebody in your audience is talking with a colleague or a friend after the meeting. The other person says, "What was that conversation about?" What would you want them to say and with what kind of energy?

We've seen so many people answer this question from their own perspective by saying something like, "They'll believe we're an essential partner" or "He'll believe I'm ready to take on a management role." Check your answers by asking, "Does this align with what *they* care about?"

As Frank continued to work on his desired outcome, he avoided this trap because he understood Jackie's role in the budget process and had just done the work to uncover what Jackie cared about. "Jackie will believe that the budget we're recommending is necessary to show the firm's commitment to sustainability, and that we're investing in projects that will make a difference. She'll feel proud to be a part of that work. And she'll approve our budget request."

3. HOW WILL YOUR AUDIENCE BENEFIT?

If your audience does what you want them to do at the end of the conversation or meeting, what positive outcome can they expect? What would make them sit up and pay attention to what you have to say during the rest of the conversation or meeting? What would get them excited? When answering the question, think of the benefit to the individual and also to the broader group or organization. In important conversations, the benefit is often far-reaching.

When considering what would happen if Jackie approved the full budget, Frank wrote, "Sustainability is an important part of our long-term strategy. The firm would benefit by becoming an industry leader in this area. Research shows that people are increasingly considering environmental commitment when deciding where to invest their money, so raising our profile would have a positive impact on customer acquisition and revenue. And Jackie would personally benefit because her values are aligned with the work we're doing."

WRITING YOUR DESIRED OUTCOME

Once you've answered these three questions, it's time to set your desired outcome. **It should be concise—just two or three sentences—and compelling.** Often, you'll want to open a conversation or meeting with it, so practice saying it out loud and get feedback when appropriate. Consider how you'll end on a note of contribution and service by coming back around to the benefit for your audience.

You can use this approach for any kind of meeting or conversation to improve your impact and results. For instance, when you work on your desired outcome for a regularly scheduled meeting, it might change how you approach it. You could turn a team status meeting into an interactive conversation designed to inspire and motivate. When you work on a desired outcome for a conversation with your kids, they're more likely to feel your respect and empathy and be open to listening. One of our participants used this approach before talking to her eighth grader about dating and told us she couldn't believe how well the conversation went.

Frank found that this was true in his conversation with Jackie. Because he had prepared well, he went into it excited rather than resigned. He told us how he started the meeting: "Jackie, I know that you care about resource sustainability, especially water conservation. My intention for this meeting is that you believe the projects we plan to invest in are smart choices that will make a difference. They'll help the company become a leader in sustainability *and* attract customers who are making investment decisions based on their environmental values. If you consider the budget from that perspective, I think you'll agree it's a reasonable request."

Frank didn't get 100 percent of the budget he had requested, but he got a *much* higher percentage than the committee had ever gotten before—and he had built a connection with a senior leader who could be their champion.

EXAMPLE OF A DESIRED OUTCOME FOR A MANAGER CONVERSATION

(My manager keeps canceling our one-on-one meetings.)

1. Who is your audience and what do they care about?
   My manager. He wants engaged employees who produce results. He wants to be known as an effective coach and get good manager effectiveness scores.

2. At the end of the conversation, what will they believe, feel, and do?
   My manager will believe that showing up for our biweekly one-on-one is key to unlocking my potential and impact. He'll feel excited by my genuine interest in his coaching. He'll commit to making these meetings a priority and not canceling or rescheduling them.

3. How will your audience benefit?
   He will recognize the value of coaching top talent and showing people that he cares about their growth. Improving my productivity and results will benefit the company. This will result in him getting a higher manager effectiveness score.

4. **Write the desired outcome** — as you might say it.

    I value your coaching. Our one-on-one meetings have helped me overcome challenges, prioritize, and brainstorm ideas. My intention today is that you see the benefit of making them a priority. I'll have an even bigger impact on our business if I can get your undivided attention and coaching for thirty minutes a week.

DESIRED OUTCOMES CAN HELP YOU TACKLE UNCOMFORTABLE CONVERSATIONS

When Raf began writing his vision, he was in the middle of a difficult relationship. His wife, Allison, could barely stand to be in the same room as his brother's wife, Gina. Without getting into years of history, let's just say she was tired of feeling insulted, judged, and unwanted. As is often the case in families, they had never addressed the issue directly with Gina or with Raf's brother, Evan.

Raf was paying a high price. He and Evan had always been close, but now they rarely saw each other. When they did, it was awkward. There was a massive elephant in the room. Raf also wasn't spending the kind of time with his niece and nephew that he would like. He was ready for it to be different and had written in his vision, "Evan and I are close, and our families spend relaxed, low-drama time together." One of the first steps Raf and his wife took was to examine the "story" they had about Gina and choose a new perspective. It helped, but it didn't solve some of the underlying problems. Even though you can't count on people to change, you can ask to be treated the way you want to be treated.

Raf knew that the only way forward was to be direct with Evan, but knew he needed to approach the conversation in a way that didn't make Evan immediately defensive. He put himself in Evan's shoes, looking at the situation from his perspective. Then he worked on setting a desired outcome.

RAF'S DESIRED OUTCOME EXAMPLE

1. Who is your audience and what do they care about?
    Evan wants a close relationship with me. He wants his kids to have a close, meaningful relationship with their only uncle.

2. What will they believe, feel, and as a result, do?
    Evan will be relieved that we're finally getting the issue on the table rather than continuing to avoid it. He'll believe Allison and I are committed to having a close relationship with him and Gina. He'll speak to Gina about our concerns and our goal of working toward a different future together.

3. How will your audience benefit?
    We'll restore our relationship as brothers and have more fun, relaxed time together. His kids will have an involved uncle and aunt, and large family gatherings will be enjoyable.

Feeling prepared to have an uncomfortable conversation, Raf called Evan and suggested they go out for coffee. Once they were seated, this is what he said: "Evan, from my perspective the relationship between our families isn't as close as either of us would like it to be. We've been avoiding the issue for too long, and if we keep going like this, our relationship will keep suffering. Allison and I are both committed to doing what it takes to resolve the issues. My intention is that you leave here willing to talk to Gina about improving this relationship. It would be amazing to have fun together as couples, to have more time with your kids, and to feel connected as brothers."

Years later, when telling us this story, Raf said, "It was a *really* powerful moment." Considering the conversation and situation from Evan's perspective gave him the confidence to address it, and helped Evan be open to it. The four of them began to make progress together. Gina hadn't realized that some of her behaviors had been such an issue. They were able to have an open discussion because they wanted the same things. The two women were never going to become best friends, but the relationship improved, the families spent more time together, and Raf and Evan felt close again.

Is there a difficult or important conversation you're postponing because you aren't sure how to approach it? Setting a desired outcome can make all the difference. In the following pages, we've shared a few more examples of conversations that can be tough to tackle or that are important enough to get right the first time.

Setting a desired outcome is the first step toward conversations and meetings that help you take ground and make progress toward your vision. Once you have defined it, you're ready to plan the rest of the conversation so that it supports that outcome. In the next chapter, we'll give you the tools to make it happen.

Chapter 13

HOW TO MAKE EVERY CONVERSATION COUNT

James walked into the small conference room and dove in. He was meeting with the product team to get them on board with his marketing plan and the timeline they would need to adhere to. It was a hard to get these five people together given their crowded schedules, and the stakes for James were high. If he could get their buy-in, the plan could move forward, ensuring his team's success on the new product rollout. If not, it could result in delays and confusion. That wouldn't look good for him.

He opened with his desired outcome for the meeting, and everybody seemed engaged. About ten minutes into his presentation, though, he could tell he was losing the room. People looked increasingly checked out, and he felt like he was rambling rather than making clear points. One of his colleagues raised a concern about part of the plan and James *tried* to address it, but he felt like he was floundering. When he saw their time was up and that people were shuffling papers and preparing to leave, he realized they would need *another* meeting. They hadn't gotten aligned on the plan or the timeline. He closed with a quick "Any questions?" and left feeling disappointed in himself and stressed out about the product release.

Think about a conversation or meeting you had recently that you expected to go smoothly. Suddenly, it took a turn that you didn't expect. How did you feel? How did you respond? Afterward, did you think of points you should have made but didn't? And did you regret any of the things you *did* say, or just wish you had handled the whole thing better? Even when you walk away feeling pretty good about a conversation or a presentation, are you always getting the results you want?

The solution to all of these hurdles, challenges, and hiccups is effective preparation.

>>

**If an important conversation is worth having,
it's worth preparing well to have it.**

>>

Remember, if you want to be intentional in how you communicate, you start by getting clear about the outcomes you're trying to achieve—you set a desired outcome—and then you *prepare* to make them happen. Not all preparation is the same, though. We're not talking about creating an agenda of points to cover or creating a slide deck. **We're recommending that you prepare in a way that helps you be concise, persuasive, and compelling.**

That's what our conversation planner offers. When you use it, you'll become more comfortable and confident sharing your recommendations and requests. You'll address concerns without losing momentum. You'll leave people ready to take action, moving the ball down the field. You'll get more accomplished with less effort and angst.

CONVERSATION PLANNER

1. What is the desired outcome?
    o   Who is my audience and what do they care about?

- o At the end of the conversation, what will they believe, feel, and do?
- o How will my audience benefit?

2. What specific recommendations or requests will I make? Why?
3. What questions will I ask? When?
4. What objections or concerns might come up? How will I handle them?
5. How will I close in a way that forwards action?

This level of preparation can seem time-consuming, but it saves time and effort in the long run and makes it much more likely that you'll produce the desired outcome you set. If you can do that, one conversation or meeting after another, you'll make faster progress toward the outcomes in your vision.

That's what James needed to do with his next meeting. He put time in his calendar to prepare using the conversation planner, and it made a massive difference. Everybody came away feeling aligned, committed to the plan, and clear on next steps and responsibilities. That's the kind of clarity, confidence, and results that good preparation can give you. James began preparing this way for every important conversation and meeting and it helped him be more intentional and effective.

Participants in our workshops have told us they've used the conversation planner to gain alignment on important initiatives, grow business, manage up and down, resolve conflict with colleagues, nail job interviews, and request resources and investment. Outside of work, they've used it to navigate important conversations about committing to a relationship, the birds and the bees, advocating for a cause they support, and so much more. (Wendy used it to talk to her teenaged kids about dating!)

In the rest of this chapter, we'll walk you through our planner so that you can move from talking *at* people to having engaged, interactive conversations. We'll help you identify disempowering language that diminishes your impact. And we'll address the super important step of *practicing*! Our goal is to help you communicate with confidence and intention, because it smooths the way to the life you want.

USING THE CONVERSATION PLANNER

When Mei received her annual performance review with her pay increase, she was surprised—and not positively. With a possible increase of 4 to 7 percent for her performance tier, she expected at least 6 percent and maybe 7. She had gotten 4.5.

The issue was complicated. Mei's manager, Jason, was new, coming on board just two months earlier. Mei worked hard and felt that she was doing good work, but the results weren't there yet. She was working on a line of business that was fairly new for the company, and the kind of work she did was more measurable with established products. It was also really important work to do in advance of the product launch, but she couldn't point to great outcomes yet. And Jason didn't know her or understand her role on the team well.

If this had happened a year before, Mei would have said nothing. She had a long-standing habit of avoiding conflict and not calling attention to herself, especially with people higher in the org chart. This tendency partially stemmed from her upbringing and Chinese cultural background. A week after receiving her review, Mei was sitting in a Fast Forward session focused on language of action. When asked the question we posed in chapter eleven—*Where would it make a difference to be on the field?*—she went to work on this situation.

Mei told us that when she was done working through the conversation planner, she couldn't believe how competent and calm she felt. "I had no fears or negative emotions about having the conversation with my manager. It felt simple, just an open conversation with another human being." The conversation she had with Jason ended up changing the course of her career.

But we're jumping ahead. Let's look at how she used the questions to prepare. For this conversation, she used all of them, but you might not need to address every question for every conversation or meeting you have. Use the ones that are relevant. Be thoughtful and intentional with your answers. And start using it right away.

1. What is the desired outcome?

We spent an entire chapter on this question because it's the most important. We won't rehash that content except to say that beginning with a desired outcome will help you consider who your audience is, why they should care, and at the end of the conversation, what they'll believe, feel, and do. **Opening the meeting or conversation by sharing the desired outcome, or at least some aspects of it, is a powerful way to start.** It sets the tone and the focus.

When you think about how you'll start, keep this in mind: People have a lot going on. They're often not listening (more on that challenge in the next Power Principle). Maybe you're meeting number four in their day. You need to get their attention in the first few minutes and give them a reason to engage. Imagine that the person you're talking to has a sticky note on their forehead that says, "Why should I care? How can you help me? Why should I put my phone down?"

Mei knew one important fact about Jason: he cared about performing well in his new role, achieving the team goals, and being seen as an effective leader. She leveraged this when writing a desired outcome:

My intention is that you leave appreciating my contributions and the unique value I bring to this team and especially our biggest product launch. As a result, you'll advocate for a higher salary increase for me.

Taking that step and considering the situation from Jason's perspective gave her a boost of confidence and greater clarity on the rest of the conversation.

2. What specific recommendations or requests will I make? Why?

Two things make for a strong recommendation or request:

- It should be concise, something you can say in one or two sentences.
- It should be well-supported and compelling. As you consider the "why," what examples, insights, evidence, case studies, or data should you share? Be careful that you don't overload your audience and end up moving off the field. All you need is the essential information that supports the specific request or recommendation.

When you get to the point in the conversation when you have to actually make your recommendation or request, it can be easy to stumble, hesitate, or start to ramble. Practice saying your recommendations or requests out loud and practice with others when it makes sense to get their feedback. You'll be prepared to be clear, concise, and *confident* in the moment.

Mei wrote

I'm requesting a salary increase of 6.5 percent rather than 4.5.

Then she made a list of supporting points or information she would share.

- Examples of praise from past managers and other leaders for my specific contributions to the rollout strategy
- Spearheaded a cross-department program for reviewing customer feedback
- Trained the team on new tools in our project management software
- New salary would be aligned with the current market rate for people in my role (show comparative data)

3. What questions will I ask? When?

Heading into important conversations prepared with questions about your audience's concerns and challenges is key. A strategic question can sometimes change the outcome of a conversation, especially when there's potential misalignment. It's helpful to write your questions down and consider *when* you'll ask them—when you need specific information or when you need your audience to pay attention and engage.

Mei realized that she didn't have much insight into how salary increases were set, or if her new manager had a different mindset about the process than her previous manager. She decided that before she made her recommendation for a specific salary increase, she would ask

> *Other than what's in my performance review, what factors influenced the decision about my salary increase?*

4. What objections might come up? How will I handle them?

When people raise objections and we aren't sure how to respond, our stress level rises and we become less effective communicators. Getting out in front of objections by appreciating and planning to address them is a much better strategy than hoping they won't come up or dismissing them as irrelevant. If there *is* an objection, wouldn't you rather address it than leave your audience to discuss it when you aren't around? You might even raise it before they do, saying something like, "You may be concerned about X. Here's another perspective." However you decide to handle objections, being prepared will help you leave people feeling clear and confident in your recommendation or request.

Mei expected that Jason's most obvious objection would be

> *The team hasn't hit its goals, which means less budget for raises.*

However, she knew they were on-target to release the new product in a month, and because a competitor was struggling, the revenue projections had actually increased by 20 percent. She felt more confident knowing she could raise that as a supporting point if necessary. She was also prepared to suggest a bonus, based on a successful product release, rather than a salary increase.

5. How will I close in a way that forwards action?

Too often, our important meetings or conversations peter out at the end. We throw up a slide that says "Thank you," or we ask, "Do you have any questions?" or say, "Let's regroup next week." When people don't respond, we wrap things up and move on. We don't save time to find out what got heard. This is your opportunity to get feedback, address concerns and additional objections, and align on actions to be taken. Here are some suggestions:

Find out what got heard. Allocate time at the end of the meeting to ask open-ended questions (rather than yes/no questions): What are you taking away from this conversation? What are your thoughts on this recommendation or request? How do these ideas fit with your overall plan? How do you want to move forward?

Reinforce the benefit of taking the action you suggested, or the risk of not doing so. Bring the conversation back around to the desired outcome, being concise and clear.

Align on *who is doing what by when.* We're often vague at the end of meetings and don't align on specific action items to be handled by specific people. Sometimes we say "we" when talking about next steps. Who is "we"? Don't leave people, including yourself, spinning and unsure of what to do next. Don't lose the momentum you've created by getting on the field in the meeting. Within twenty-four hours, follow up in writing on actions and agreements.

Mei wasn't sure what she would hear in the meeting with Jason, so wasn't entirely sure how she would close. She decided the most important thing she could do was determine his alignment with and commitment to her request.

- Ask: How can we close the gap?
- If he needs time to get an answer, ask: What's the process and timeline for getting approval?
- If he says no, ask: Can we revisit the topic after the product release?

Getting on the Field

After taking the time to prepare for what could have been an uncomfortable conversation, Mei felt calm and confident. She was ready to get on the field and set a meeting with Jason. She kicked things off by sharing her desired outcome. Then, she asked about factors influencing the salary increase, and Jason told her that all salary increases for the year were a bit lower because of concerns about market conditions. He also acknowledged that he hadn't done a good job of making that clear to the team. She decided to ask for 6 percent rather than 6.5. She walked Jason through the examples and data to support her request and concluded by asking how they could close the gap.

Jason's response was interesting: "Wow, you're well prepared . . . I'm not." He asked for time to speak to HR and senior leaders about her request. She asked for a timeline and he told her he would have an answer by the end of the next week. We'd love to tell you that Mei then got a nice pay raise. That didn't happen. The company had finalized its budget and the leaders weren't willing to reconsider any increases.

Here's what *did* happen, though. When Jason shared the news, he said, "I really appreciate the kind of courage you showed in our conversation. You advocated for yourself so well, I think you can do it for others. I'm going to start looking for management roles for you." Six months later, with

Jason's support, Mei was promoted to lead a team of her own in another department—and got a salary increase with the position.

CONVERSATION PLANNER EXAMPLE: REQUESTING A BIGGER BUDGET

1. What is the desired outcome?

   My intention is that you see the impact of the two new projects signed this month on our team's workload. I know you care about meeting promised deadlines and preventing team burnout. I'd like your support in hiring outside support to make sure both things happen.

2. What specific recommendations or requests will I make? Why?

   My request is that you approve hiring one new independent contractor to provide writing support.
   o The most time-consuming work for these projects will be writing, and it is the easiest to outsource.
   o Hiring a contractor will allow us to be flexible, using only the time and budget we need to complete the work.
   o Show timesheet summary of employees who are at close to max capacity on existing projects

3. What questions will I ask? When?

   Ask before addressing budget objection: Do you know of any other projects in the pipeline that could affect our workload?

4. What objections might come up? How will I handle them?

   You might be thinking that getting approval for this hire means reporting a budget overage to Jeff and Sarah, which

I understand puts you and the team in an awkward position. However, the two new projects put us on track to surpass our revenue projections for the year by at least 15 percent. I anticipate that the cost of the contractor will increase our budget by only 5 percent. I've also been able to find an excellent contractor without going through a recruiter or other service, which has saved us money.

5. How will I close in a way that forwards action?
   o What are you saying to yourself about this request? (Find out what got heard.)
   o To avoid falling behind, we need to bring the contractor on by the end of next week.
   o Do you need to get approval before I can send an agreement to the contractor? If so, can that happen by Friday?

STOP USING LANGUAGE THAT LIMITS YOUR IMPACT

Preparing for your conversations matters, especially when they are important. If you want to have an even greater impact in the moment, we recommend you raise your consciousness of how you typically speak, because your unconscious habits might be *diminishing* your impact. As a first step, consider this list of common ineffective habits and highlight any that resonate.

- **Cut disclaimers:** Phrases like "You might already know this," "This may not be the right idea," "I didn't get much time to spend on this," or "This may be a stupid question" make us seem less confident and create doubt when there shouldn't be any.

- **Stop apologizing:** Apologizing when you've done nothing wrong undermines your credibility and power. Without thinking about it, we say, "Sorry for taking up so much of your time" or "I'm sorry we don't have the final data" or "Sorry, can I borrow a phone charger?" If this sounds like you, it's time to stop. Only apologize when a sincere apology is necessary.

- **Eliminate "just":** Adding "just" before we say what we're going to do makes it seem small or unimportant, as in "I'm just going to share this data" or "I just want to tell you about an idea I had." Notice when you are saying "just" and eliminate it!

- **Be concise:** Being concise is always more powerful. When we're not, it can seem like we're piling it on or "overproving" our point. For instance, "I know you will agree with my point about our strategy, which I have discussed and debated at length with my team, although it's really a pretty unarguable plan and very straightforward" versus "My team's new strategic plan is X, Y, Z." This is a deluge of words that ends up meaning nothing; the point is buried. Being concise simply requires preparation—time to distill your thoughts and determine how to express them best.

- **Tell rather than ask:** If you have a recommendation, make it clearly and confidently rather than asking for it. For instance, "Let's set a time to review our proposal next week" instead of "Can we schedule a time to review our proposal next week?" Or "I recommend we test this idea" rather than "What do you think about testing this idea?" Also, avoid raising your pitch at the end of a statement, making it *sound* like a question.

- **Use "and" rather than "but":** Substituting "and" for "but" will avoid disempowering people and putting them on the defensive. You want them open to your ideas and feedback. For instance, "I appreciate your insights, *but* we have another perspective" versus "I appreciate your insights, *and* we have another perspective."

- **Reduce filler words:** Often, we fill time and gaps in our line of thought with words and phrases like "to be honest," "um," "uh," "like," "actually," "sort of," "kind of," "you know," "right," or "by the way." It makes us seem hesitant and unsure of ourselves or our ideas. Slowing down and pausing will help you to use fewer filler words. Try it. You'll be amazed at how much improvement you'll see in a short time.

PRACTICE, PRACTICE, PRACTICE

Athletes have access to a helpful tool for continuous improvement: They're often filmed when they're competing or playing. Afterward, they watch the film and examine what worked and what they could do better. Most of us have no film to turn to. If we want to become better communicators, it's up to us to make the effort to assess our performance and work on continuous improvement.

It begins by practicing—out loud. Language and delivery *both* matter. Preparing an outline using the conversation planner will improve your confidence and impact, and practicing allows you to work on cutting out disempowering language, overcoming a tendency to ramble, and showing up with the right energy.

Research has shown the high impact of our facial expressions, tone, and body language on how people perceive what we're saying. Tone is especially important in conversations or meetings where tensions might be high, where alignment may be off, or where emotions could run deep. When you practice out loud, you neutralize the emotions that come with high-stakes conversations. Practicing can help you overcome the story running through your head about how the conversation will go and how people will receive what you have to say—because your mindset may not be as advanced or refined as your language. If you let anger, frustration, or anxiety come through in your delivery, the words you say won't matter much.

If you can practice with another person who will give you candid feedback, great. If not, try recording yourself and then watching the video.

Fine-tune your timing, tone, even your facial expressions so you can speak with confidence and conviction.

After the meeting or conversation, debrief alone or with other people. The three questions we recommend for any debrief are:

- What worked well? (Start with the positive!)
- What didn't work and why?
- What can I learn from this or how can I improve?

At Fast Forward, even though we've been delivering some of our workshops for close to a decade, we still take time to debrief after every one. And we always find something to improve, even if it's small. Small improvements make a massive difference over time.

Imagine what would be possible in the coming week or month if you were effectively and efficiently influencing and inspiring others with every conversation or meeting. When you use our conversation planner, that's what happens. Try it this week, and then keep practicing. You will be amazed by how fast your communication improves.

In the next Power Principle, we'll focus on the other aspect of communication—listening. We'll explore how listening can be a superpower that deepens relationships, helps you have a positive impact on others, and frees you from solving other people's problems.

STOP TALKING AND GET CURIOUS

Spark Connection, Trust, and Creativity

Chapter 14

THE PROFOUND IMPACT OF LISTENING + CURIOSITY

Lisa: Years ago, my husband, Sean, and I were both working full-time and had three tween kids. Every night when we got home, I would ask, "How was your day?" Before he could answer the question, I was across the room cleaning up and directing the kids on dinner and homework. One night, Sean got tired of it. "Don't ask me how my day was if you don't care enough to listen," he said.

I knew immediately that he was right. It was unconscious, but I wasn't listening. Then he added, "If only I was your client, because you certainly give them your undivided attention. You hang on their every word." He had a fair point.

"I just don't know that much about your industry," I said. This was maybe not the best response.

"Well, first thing, we don't call it an industry." Sean was a police officer.

That night, I committed to giving Sean the same level of *intentional* listening I gave to my clients and colleagues. (Not every day—let's be real.) I began by slowing down, holding still, and looking at him when he told me about his day. After almost two decades together, I found that I was learning new things about his job, the people he worked with, and the challenges he faced.

I got curious and asked questions, some of which were the kinds of things I would ask a client: What does success look like at the end of the year? What are you measured on? What are people frustrated by? Over time, Sean started sharing more and more about his work. He would show me an interesting YouTube video or include me on an email chain with his colleagues about a Dilbert cartoon. All of a sudden, I was part of the conversation. One day, I said to him, jokingly, "I love being part of the Nassau County Police Department."

And he said to me, *seriously*, "Well, now you're listening. Now you care."

Lisa's story is typical. It's very human to let almost everything get in the way of listening and getting curious. When that happens, we're cut off from deeper relationships, from ideas that could propel us forward, and from the benefits of allowing other people to think out loud—all of which can help us achieve outcomes in our visions.

Listening and getting curious are key to making your vision a reality.

First, intentional listening improves the quality of your relationships—which improves the quality of your life. Most people don't feel heard, so listening is one of the greatest gifts you can give them. When you do, you have the power to profoundly influence their thinking and their emotional state.

You encourage them to explore their ideas, which helps them become more creative and innovative. You build trust and connection. You improve collaboration and their commitment to supporting you.

When answering the vision question "What do you want to be known for?" people often write things like "being an inspirational leader," "being a loving parent," "being someone who takes a stand," or "being someone who empowers people." Every one of those becomes more possible with intentional listening.

Practically, being an intentional listener forwards action. You learn things that you wouldn't have known otherwise and discover ideas that can make all the difference. When you're curious, you make better decisions because you are more fully informed and more aware of other perspectives. Listening and getting curious give you access to a whole world of knowledge you don't possess and opens doors you didn't even know existed, putting your vision within reach.

Developing strong listening skills takes awareness and practice because we aren't taught to do it well. Our general human-ness gets in the way in the form of impatience, busyness, self-interest, or distraction. In this chapter, we're going to help you understand how to overcome those hurdles and the incredible benefits for you and everybody in your life when you do. We'll offer tips for quieting your inner chatter and generating curiosity at will so that people feel heard and sense your interest rather than your distraction or boredom. And we'll offer coaching and exercises for practicing your intentional listening.

You can improve with attention and practice—and immediately improve your communication, leadership, results, and *progress on your vision.*

OUR DEFAULT: UNCONSCIOUS LISTENING

Think about a conversation you've had in the last couple of days with a colleague, a friend, or your partner. Try to remember how it went. Remember what they were sharing or the story they were telling you. As they were talking, what were you thinking about? If they were sharing a challenge in their relationship or at work, were you thinking about your own similar challenges or teeing up the solution that was so obvious to you? If they were telling you about their job, vacation, or puppy, were you waiting to tell them about your job, vacation, or puppy? Were you waiting—maybe impatiently—to chime in and share your experience or ideas?

Try to remember what happened next. If the conversation went the way of most conversations, you might have interrupted to share your own experience or to tell them what you thought they should do. You might have waited for them to finish but then taken them on a tangent, away from their point or story, toward a topic that you wanted to talk about. You were probably listening to them the way most of us listen most of the time—through a filter:

- To reply or make our own point
- To relate it back to our experience and knowledge, so that we can contribute or add value
- To confirm what we already knew or our assumptions
- To find opportunities to be smart, to have the right answer, to be an expert
- To solve or fix a problem

Now imagine that that person was trying to tell you something deeply important—because they might have been. You'll never know because they never got the chance.

Like the rest of us, Jack was listening to the people in his life through these filters. When he was growing up, the phrase "silence is golden" was definitely *not* his family's motto. At the dinner table, everybody was expected to talk, contribute, and respond to questions. His mother would literally say, "What's wrong? Why are you so quiet?" if he wasn't talking. At school, he was expected to talk less, but he was also taught *how* to listen: He should be thinking about how he would respond if he was called on, or he should be making a connection between what he was learning and his own experiences. When he got to college, he was often graded on how much he contributed to the class discussion or how many of his ideas were incorporated into group projects. And as he began his career in sales, 90 percent of his training was on what to say and how to say it, especially ways to "add value" and be seen as "a problem solver."

Given all this "training," the feedback from Jack's team during a review shouldn't have been a surprise: They all said he was a lousy listener. During a session with a Fast Forward coach discussing the feedback and his listening habits, he had a small breakthrough. "I'm always jumping in," he said. "Without letting other people even finish their sentence, I think I have the answer or that I have to solve for something in real time rather than sitting quietly, digesting, listening to everything they have to say."

It's not that Jack or any of us are completely self-absorbed or don't care about the people in our lives. We're simply unconscious, busy, and distracted. **We're not present.** We're moving fast and thinking about so many things that we're skimming the surface of what's happening in front of us.

Because *we* rarely feel heard, we can be impatient to talk about something we're interested in or knowledgeable about. In her book *You're Not Listening*, Kate Murphy points to a sadly hilarious *New Yorker* cartoon of a cocktail party as a perfect example of this. One guy holding a glass of wine says, "Behold, as I guide our conversation to my narrow area of expertise."[1]

Often, we want to be of service. We want to add value, so we listen for an opportunity to share an idea or solution. And we tend to operate on the assumption that we already know what the person is going to say. We end up mentally jumping ahead in the conversation, missing out of what's being said in the moment. **We also think we're *expected* to contribute in some way in *every* conversation.** If we aren't, it feels uncomfortable or like we aren't doing our job or fulfilling our role. This can be especially true for managers and for parents.

Our ineffective listening habits come with a high cost. When people don't feel heard, they withdraw, clam up, and are less willing to be transparent or vulnerable. They can become defensive in response to what we have to say because the conversation feels one-sided. This can take an enormous toll on connection and trust, especially with the people we care about the most.

Poor listening can limit creativity and innovative thinking and narrow the possibilities in every aspect of our life and work. We cut people's thinking off just when they're getting to the good stuff—the most important ideas or the root of a challenge. For instance, when we're working on communication with sales teams, one of the most common complaints we hear is, "We ask the client lots of questions, but they're so tight lipped. We get very little information out of them." We say, "Maybe it has something to do with how you're listening. Are you showing them that you actually care about the answers—or do they feel you're just asking questions for show?" In all aspects of life, but especially in business, **when people trust that you're not going to "pivot and pounce," using whatever they say to support your proposal or argument or agenda, they'll be more open** *and* **more willing to listen to** *you.*

Like Lisa, Jack was given a gift. Somebody made him aware of the impact of his unconscious listening habits. Many of us never get this chance. When Jack changed how he was listening, the results were profound.

IMPROVING HOW YOU LISTEN TRANSFORMS YOUR LIFE AND WORK

Jack's inability to listen effectively was showing up throughout his life. At least once a week, something at home slipped through the cracks and his wife would say, "I told you about that two days ago!" He had received feedback from his boss that in meetings, he needed to be more analytical and thoughtful in his comments. It wasn't until his team raised the issue and described how *un*heard they felt in his review that Jack started to connect the dots. In one meeting after another, he recognized how often he was drifting away from the discussion, focusing on his next meeting or task or on some point he wanted to be sure to make. And he realized the impact this behavior was having on his relationships at home—his family was exasperated.

Step by step, he began to practice the skills we'll share in this chapter and the next. He worked on being more present, on eliminating distractions when people were speaking to him, on overcoming his inner chatter. The results were profound. First, when members of his team came to him to discuss challenges they were facing, he worked on *only* listening rather than jumping to the end of the conversation and handing them a solution. He found they were usually able to get to the solution on their own if he gave them a chance. His conversations with his wife became deeper and more productive, and they argued less. It helped that he wasn't forgetting about family activities so often. At work, he felt more informed because he was listening better in meetings. He was also able to offer better insights and feedback in group conversations, partially because he waited for people to share all the details without interrupting them.

"Listening—intentionally—is so powerful," he said recently. "If you do it consistently, you can learn so much." While he's not perfect and has to work on it every day, becoming a better listener transformed every aspect of Jack's life.

The most important first step on the road to being an intentional listener is understanding the incredible value of listening—for others and for you, the listener. Being listened to affects how we feel and how we think. When we put our negative emotions into words, those feelings can lessen in intensity (as long as we're not simply repeating complaints over and over).[2] When we have good listeners in their lives, we have greater "cognitive resilience," or better mood and memory.[3]

In her powerful book *Time to Think: Listening to Ignite the Human Mind*, Nancy Kline explains that if you want to improve people's thinking, give them your full attention. Listen at the highest level and ask incisive questions. She was inspired by the first excellent listener in her life: "My mother's listening was not ordinary. Her attention was so immensely dignifying, her expression so seamlessly encouraging, that you found yourself thinking clearly in her presence, suddenly understanding what before had been confusing, finding a brand-new, surprising idea. You found excitement where there had been tedium. You faced something. You solved a problem. You felt good again . . . She simply gave attention. But the quality of that attention was catalytic."[4]

Do you think the people in your life feel this way after talking to you? If they did, the benefits would be profound. When you make the effort to be an intentional listener, the dynamics of your important relationships improve. When people feel your empathy through your attention, how they engage with you changes. A little empathy goes a long way to creating trust and connection, especially in relationships that are fraught or even adversarial.

It's a limiting belief that you're too busy or don't have enough time to listen. When you *take* the time, you become known for being supportive and receptive to ideas. You almost always save time in the long run, because you have access to ideas, information, and perspectives that could improve your progress toward your vision.

EXERCISE: WHERE COULD YOU IMPROVE YOUR LISTENING?

- What specific hurdles get in the way of listening for you? Think of certain situations where you know you're less intentional.
- What's the cost of not listening in these situations?
- What could be possible if you listened intentionally?

HOW TO LISTEN INTENTIONALLY

Consistent, intentional listening requires self-management—which takes discipline, rigor, and practice. This is especially true because our conversations are almost never a one-way flow of information. Sometimes, you *do* need to contribute. Sometimes, people are looking for specific help or advice. If you think about listening as a pendulum, though, most of us spend too much time all the way on the "sort of listening" side. The opposite side is "intense listening" where you're doing nothing but letting somebody talk. Sometimes that's appropriate, but more often, you'll be somewhere in the middle. Intentional listening is thoughtful and appropriate for the circumstances.

No matter what kind of conversation you are having or your role in it, though, the listening strategies required don't change.

Slow everything down. The biggest hurdle to listening is our ability to focus. Amazingly, we have the ability to shift our brain function in the moment with one simple technique: slower, deeper breathing, especially in through the nose. This increases the alpha waves in our brains, which relaxes us; increases activity in the parts of the brain that make us alert, pleasant, and analytical; and reduces activity in the parts associated with anxiety, anger, and confusion.[5] You can slow your thinking down and improve your focus simply by changing your breathing. Pair that with actively relaxing your body and slowing your movements to show up as calm and attentive.

Be fully present. Get rid of distractions and don't try to multitask. If you are easily distracted during conversations by the presence of your phone, put it aside. At the beginning of every workshop we lead, we ask participants to take a couple of minutes and talk to somebody else in the room about anything on their mind that could distract them from being present. You can do this on your own in advance of an important conversation. Sometimes it helps to write out a few notes to clear any mental clutter.

Show you're engaged and open with your body language. Face the person you're talking to and make eye contact. When we look at people during conversations, our mirror neurons kick in and we become more attuned to their intentions and emotions. Our brain waves also sync up. But that doesn't happen if we're not looking at each other![6] And never forget the power of nonverbal cues. Research has found that they account for more than 60 percent of the meaning the other person takes away from the interaction, and when they match up with what you're actually saying, they increase trust. *Show* you're listening by leaning in rather than crossing your arms and leaning back. Neutralize your expression, especially if it's an emotional or stressful conversation or meeting. (We'll have more to say on paying attention to the other person's body language in the next chapter.)

Don't interrupt or take the person on a tangent. If you have questions or ideas as they're talking that you don't want to forget, consider taking a short note or two to remind yourself, and then refocus.

Ask open-ended questions. Prompt them to share more or go deeper with questions like "Can you tell me more about that?" or "What's exciting/important about that for you?"

If you check out (and you probably will), notice it and check back in. Be honest, especially if you missed something. Ask them to repeat what they said. If you keep checking out because something is distracting you, ask them to pause for a moment, take a note about whatever it is that's getting in your way, and then ask them to go on.

These methods sound straightforward, but intentional listening isn't easy. The best thing to do is to start immediately and keep practicing. The Discovery Challenge, shared next, is the exercise we use with participants to strengthen their listening muscle. Use it today and see what you learn—about yourself and somebody else.

EXERCISE: THE DISCOVERY CHALLENGE

Pick one person in your life who could use your full attention or who you would like to build a stronger connection with. It could be a friend, a family member, a colleague, or your boss. You'll engage them in a five-minute conversation on something *they're* passionate about and that you don't know much about, like their favorite movie, a vacation they're planning, a book they are reading—anything that will get them talking.

- Right before you begin the conversation, reread the list of practices we described to help you focus on intentional listening.
- Ask the person a question that gets them talking about the topic.
- As they talk, do not interrupt, relate what they're sharing back to your own experiences, or take them on a tangent away from what they seem to want to share. Only prompt them to go deeper with open-ended questions.
- Use all of the intentional listening practices we shared on the previous page, especially making sure to notice when you check out. Also try to notice how often you're tempted to do any of the things you're not supposed to do.
- After the conversation, debrief by considering these questions: How hard was it? What did you learn that you didn't know? What was your interest level in what they were sharing? How were they different at the end of the conversation? What's one thing you need to work on?

GROWING YOUR CURIOSITY

Who are the most curious people on the planet? Small children. Their curiosity knows no limits. They carry a sense of wonder about the world and the people in it. They ask a million questions. But as people get older, we lose our sense of wonder. We become uncomfortable showing enthusiasm or interest. We become enmeshed in "knowing" rather than "learning." This perspective limits our engagement with the world and especially with people. We can fool ourselves into thinking that they can't sense our lack of interest, but they can.

We can practice the skills of listening and become better at them, but **to be a master listener, we also have to develop our ability to be curious at will.** You can get curious about anything if you overcome the three biggest hurdles.

The first is our mindset. How often have you been presented with an opportunity to explore something—watch a movie or show, attend an event, go on some outing—and you replied, "I'm not interested in that." We tend to relate to our level of interest as black and white, as something out of our control. We find something interesting or we don't. If we don't, there's no point in exposing ourselves to it. In fact, we can change our level of interest in almost anything. More than likely, if you think you aren't interested, you may not *know* enough to be interested, which brings us to the next hurdle.

The second hurdle is that we check out. This may seem like a chicken-and-the-egg argument, but becoming more curious begins with better listening. When we listen enough to learn a little information, our brain goes to work incorporating what we learned into what we already know. That process highlights gaps in our knowledge, which makes us wonder what we're missing. Think back to Lisa's story at the beginning of the chapter. She didn't start off being interested in the inner workings of a police department, but as she listened intentionally to Sean, she learned just enough for the gaps in her understanding to motivate her to get curious. The more curious she got, the better a listener she became.

The third major hurdle to curiosity is the assumption that we already know or should know. The cure is reminding yourself that curiosity is how you access the massive world of knowledge you've never even touched. Within that world are ideas that could help you achieve your vision or improve your life in some significant way.

When we work to overcome these hurdles, the benefits are huge. Wendy was recently on a video call with Tom, one of our coaches, who was telling her about a coaching certification he had just completed. It was a packed day for her, and she felt impatient (not a new feeling for her). She has completed certifications like Tom's before, so she wasn't really interested in what he was saying because she assumed she knew what it was all about. She was waiting for him to finish so she could move on to the next thing on her to-do list.

But seeing the enthusiasm and excitement on Tom's face triggered her to start paying attention. She forced herself to slow down and get curious. A funny thing happened when she did. She wanted more information. She had questions. The more they talked, the more curious she got. About ten minutes in, she realized that the certification he was talking about covered a whole set of coaching skills—and it could be ideal for some of our clients. There was an opportunity to expand our toolkit and help our clients grow in new areas. If she hadn't slowed down and gotten curious, she would have missed it!

As behavioral scientist Francesca Gino, author of *Rebel Talent*, writes in *Harvard Business Review*, "When our curiosity is triggered, we think more deeply and rationally about decisions and come up with more-creative solutions."[7] The research shows that when we're actively curious, we make fewer decision-making errors because we're overcoming our own natural biases, like confirmation bias and stereotyping. We're moving past the assumption that we already know. We also have more-open communication and greater collaboration, which leads to better ideas and results for people, teams, and companies.

Moving past our assumptions and getting curious also benefits us in handling conflict. A program participant, Sima, shared a powerful story. At the time, she was working in procurement and was negotiating a new contract with a vendor. Every time she got on a video call with her contact, he seemed impatient, frustrated, and unwilling to answer her questions. She was becoming equally frustrated, even angry, but she decided to get curious rather than respond in a way that could kill the deal. On their next call, when she noticed the same behaviors, she addressed them: "You seem like you have something on your mind today. Would there be a better time to have this conversation? Or would you like to share it with me?" And he did! Sadly, his father, who he was very close with, was in the hospital, and he was distraught. He was working in calls and meetings between time with his father and felt annoyed that nobody else on his team could handle these things. From then on, everything about their interactions changed.

Sima is a woman of color and was operating in an industry that was predominantly white and male. She told us that it could have been easy for her to assume her contact's behavior was being influenced by unconscious bias. It's possible that that *was* a factor. By getting curious and helping him move beyond his emotional state, though, she built a positive working relationship that helped them both succeed—and that might have had a positive impact on any unconscious bias in play.

Over and over, we say to participants who aren't getting the support, answers, or alignment they want, "Get curious. Ask why you received the answer you did. Ask other questions that could help you understand or take a different approach. And listen carefully, without assumptions." Being curious gives us the power to turn any conversation from reactive to collaborative.

Every day, you have opportunities to transform the way people think, improve the quality of their ideas, and deepen your relationships with them. All it takes is one thing done well and with intention: listening. It can be your new superpower. Where will you use it? And what difference could it make?

In the next chapter, we'll share how to leverage listening to coach the people in your life—your team members, your kids, your friends, your colleagues—helping them solve their *own* challenges and coming up with ideas for making work and life better.

Chapter 15

FREE YOURSELF FROM SOLVING OTHER PEOPLE'S PROBLEMS

Hannah had been a manager for about six months. She had been so excited going into the role, with big plans to work with her team on improving how they operated and contributed to the growth of the company. Instead, she felt like she spent all her time putting out fires. One problem or challenge would get resolved, and somebody else would show up at her door or send her an email about a new issue. It was relentless and exhausting.

Hannah felt so much pressure to help people solve problems. She thought she had to have the right answer and know the right thing to say. If she didn't, how was she adding value? She spent more and more of her time feeling annoyed with the people she had been excited to lead just a few months before, even resenting them. During a group coaching call, she said, "Why do I have to be involved in everything? Why can't they figure it out on their own?"

"Well," we asked, "have you let them?"

Shortly after, she attended our workshop on listening and had a break-through. The next week, every time somebody came to her with a problem, she only listened. It took every ounce of willpower she had not to jump in and tell them what to do, but she gritted her teeth and resisted the temptation. She practiced patience. She asked open-ended questions like, "What do you think you should do?" And a miraculous thing happened almost every time. They came up with a viable solution on their own—and often, they surprised her with a better idea than the one she would have suggested.

The next week, two of the people who came to her most often were showing up at her door less. And sometimes they had a solution or idea already worked out that they just wanted to run by her. She felt less drained by the end of the day—and she enjoyed her team more! And even though some conversations took longer, she found she had more time for other important work.

She began to recognize that allowing people the chance to think for themselves and coaching them to come to their own conclusions was a more valuable contribution—to their development and her own sanity—than giving them the answers. She kept practicing and became more disciplined. Even if the situation was urgent, even if they were in the middle of a crisis, she wouldn't immediately hand out an answer. (There are times as a manager when you have to provide an answer because of your expertise, but you can always ask questions first to give people an opportunity to think through a challenge.)

She found herself using the same approach with friends who were working on personal challenges, with her girlfriend who was struggling with career decisions, and with her niece who was having school issues. When she did, everybody—including her—came away more energized, with greater clarity, and ready to take action.

Of all our Power Principles, listening made the biggest difference in Hannah's ability to be the manager (and person) she wanted to be. Within a year, her team was one of the highest-performing in the company, and two members were promoted into leadership positions. After three years, she was leading the largest team in her office and was known as a "people whisperer."

Most of us can relate to Hannah's feeling that she needed to provide a solution or bring her expertise to bear on the situation. Sometimes, we do. But too often, we confuse *helping people* with *solving problems*. **We're programmed to believe that solving and fixing is the best way to help,** that it's how we build our own credibility and prove our value. That's only true if it's *our* problem to solve. If it isn't, we've deprived somebody of the opportunity to work out a solution, to grow their knowledge, and to stretch their creative thinking. And we almost guarantee that they're going to come to us with another problem to solve in the future. With this approach to life and work, you find you're only as good as the last problem you solved.

To paraphrase Michael Porter, one of the world's most influential management thinkers, the most powerful people expand the power of those around them. **You can empower the people in your life if you resist the temptation to try to solve their problems and instead** *coach* **them through their challenges.** When you do, you'll be surprised and delighted by their creativity, innovation, and brilliance. You'll get access to their ideas and knowledge. You'll learn things you don't know you don't know. You'll free up your time and energy. Together, you'll rise and grow and make progress.

As a leader, a parent, a friend, a member of a family or any group, **you can fuel a coaching culture,** just as Hannah did, with a few simple shifts. In this chapter, we're going to show you how. We'll explore the most important coaching practices—patience, asking questions, silence—and offer practical guidance on how to apply them. And we'll help you realize that coaching is a skill you can use in any part of your life to engage with people at a deeper level, to become known as somebody who lifts others up, and to discover all kinds of possibilities that will help you with your own vision.

THE LIFE-CHANGING IMPACT OF "WHAT DO YOU THINK?"

When two departments merged at Hugo's company, he was given responsibility for both. Before the other manager transitioned to a different role, they met to discuss the people on her team. "Fair warning, Martin is not the most engaged or motivated employee. His work is solid and he seems to like it here, but I wouldn't have great expectations for him."

Hugo knew Martin a little and could understand the comments. Martin was reserved and didn't often volunteer his thoughts. You never quite knew how interested he was. Hugo also knew that Martin would share valuable ideas in meetings, when prompted, and seemed to have a better grasp of the department data than others, especially how to explain it and extract meaningful insights from it. Contrary to the other manager's opinion, Hugo chose the perspective that Martin had untapped depths, and he was going to discover them. He would ask questions, listen, and discover what *Martin* thought about the value he could bring to the team.

Hugo started small, setting up one-on-one meetings with Martin. He asked questions about what Martin liked most about their work and what he saw as the team's greatest challenges. With every meeting, he kept peeling the onion. When Martin seemed to withdraw or become less communicative, he would change tack. What he discovered after a few weeks was a talent and passion for data visualization—or turning complex data into accessible insights and graphics that everybody can understand quickly. "I know that's not really part of my job here," Martin said during one conversation.

"Why do you think that's the case?" Hugo asked. That question got Martin talking about a problem he saw in the department regarding the breakdown of responsibilities. "How would you solve it?" Martin asked. Hugo shared a great idea for streamlining the work they did and leveraging people's talents better. Hugo gradually put Martin's ideas into action, giving him full credit, and was able to shift Martin's responsibilities to be more focused on report creation and cross-department data sharing.

Martin became a much more engaged and high-value member of the team. All it took was for Hugo to assume that Martin had something valuable to offer, ask open-ended questions, and then let Martin share in a way that was comfortable for him.

After listening, **one of the most vital coaching muscles is patience.** You have to wait for people to arrive at the answers they need on their own without leaping in to save the day. You have to resist the urge to push them toward the solution from your perspective. Your job is to listen between the lines and to ask a few choice questions. We'll show you what this looks like in the next two sections.

Patience is only possible if you assume that others have the answers to begin with. If your assumption is that eventually you'll have to give them the answer, or that any answer they come up with won't be as strong as yours, you're not coaching, you're just going through the motions. But **when you assume *they* have the answers already, your role is simply creating the time and space for them to show up as brilliant, creative, and resourceful.** When you can do that, you free yourself from solving their problems. Hugo didn't go into his conversations with Martin believing he knew how to solve Martin's "problem." He didn't even know if there *was* a problem. He assumed Martin had something to offer and could find his own path to engaging more with the team. Then he looked for opportunities to support Martin's ideas and build his confidence.

One reason this mindset is so essential is that people are often demotivated when others try to "help." In her book *How to Change*, psychologist Katy Milkman describes the revelation of a colleague who wondered why people who knew what they should do to solve a challenge weren't doing it, even though they were getting plenty of good advice:

> *Too often, we assume that the obstacle to change in others is ignorance, and so we offer advice to mend that gap. But what if the problem isn't ignorance but confidence — and our unsolicited wisdom isn't making things better but worse? . . . In giving advice, we might be inadvertently conveying to people*

that we don't think they can succeed on their own — implying
that we view them as so hopeless that two minutes of advice
will be worth more than all they've learned from attempting
to solve their own problems.[1]

What worked instead, based on a study Milkman and her colleagues conducted, was to ask people who were struggling to share their insights with others. Exploring their own ideas and knowledge brought them clarity and gave them confidence. Granting people the time and space to do that is a gift you can give. When you do, you'll reap the benefits, too!

EXERCISE: WHERE COULD YOU BE COACHING RATHER THAN SOLVING?

- Where in your life are you solving people's problems versus listening and questioning?
- What is the impact of this on your relationships and how you feel?
- What would be different if you stopped solving and started listening, getting curious, and questioning more?

ESSENTIAL COACHING STRATEGIES

When you adopt the mindset that people are resourceful and creative, you're more likely to create a safe environment for them to explore their thoughts and feelings. In *Think Again*, Adam Grant describes the research into how critical safety is: "In a series of experiments, interacting with an empathetic, nonjudgmental, attentive listener made people less anxious and defensive. They felt less pressure to avoid contradictions in their thinking, which encouraged them to explore their opinions more deeply, recognize nuances in them, and share them more openly."[2] **The safer we feel, the more comfortable we are taking risks—sharing our closely held ideas, feelings, and fears.** Effective coaching helps us be vulnerable, dreaming out loud, without worrying about the other person's doubt or cynicism.

To help people get there, consider these strategies:

- Before heading into coaching opportunities, prepare to be an intentional listener. Remember the suggestions we made in the last chapter. Make sure you're ready to be calm and present. Take a deep breath, clear your inner chatter, and make sure you're not showing up looking rushed or frazzled. Look people in the eye and make them feel that you have all the time in the world.

- Pay attention to the other person's body language or how they're expressing themselves. Listening between the lines means looking for disconnects between what the person is saying and their expression, tone of voice, or other nonverbal cues. We've all heard somebody say, "It's fine," while they're sending a clear message that they're *not* fine about it.

- When you do respond, rely on short, simple, open-ended questions, like "What was important about that?" or "Now what?" They show you're listening but won't lead the other person in a particular direction, allowing them to take the lead themselves. The more complicated the question, the more likely you're getting in the way of the other person's train of thought. We've provided a list of helpful questions toward the end of the chapter.

- Once you ask a question, don't speak until after they respond. Get comfortable with silence. Often, we ask a question that requires some thought, and when the other person doesn't answer right away, we assume they didn't hear us or don't know how to answer, so we jump in with another question or we answer our own question! Silence can be your greatest coaching tool if you embrace it.

- By the end of any coaching conversation, people should feel motivated to take action. Often that means getting a bit more granular with your questions over time to help them focus on the next specific steps or on trying one or two approaches. **You want them to map their own path forward and get excited about it so that they'll hold themselves accountable to making it happen.**

We've used these approaches professionally, of course, but also with our families, our kids, and our friends. And we're always inspired by how brilliant people can be when we give them the gift of time and space to think.

HAVING POWERFUL COACHING CONVERSATIONS

You've probably had people in your life come to you with a problem. With an outsider's perspective, you might see things that they don't. But trying to solve a problem for somebody else rushes them past the important mental steps of examining the problem carefully, considering options thoroughly, and brainstorming solutions that could work best for *them*. Let's look at an example to see how a powerful coaching conversation *could* go.

Wendy: Not long ago, I was working with a new leader, Elias. He was in conflict with a colleague, Brittany, and it was affecting his work, his attitude, and the effectiveness of his leadership. He had to work with her most days, and their teams worked together closely. Elias had already chosen a new perspective on their relationship, which helped, but there were still challenges that needed to be resolved. Specifically, they had very different ideas on some key work the teams had to collaborate on. I knew he could find his way to the right approach better than I could. I wasn't present and didn't know Brittany or any of the players involved. Even if I did, my solution wouldn't necessarily be the best solution *for him*.

Here's how our conversation went.

Elias: The situation with Brittany is still tense. She feels it, I feel it, and I can tell the team feels it.

Me: Hmm. Tell me more.

Elias: Well, every time we're together you can cut the tension with a knife. It's really awkward for everyone involved, and I can see it affecting how people perceive me as the team leader.

Me: You used the words "tense" and "tension" a few times. Can you tell me more about what that looks like?

Elias: It's clear that we don't agree on a lot of things, and when those clashes happen in front of other people, we can all feel tension mounting, like we want to start yelling at each other but we don't.

Me: What are you thinking in those moments?

Elias: That it's a big problem. That we have to come to an agreement. That I feel frustrated because I don't know how to get her to see my side. Everything feels harder than it should. I'm pretty sure she's not any happier with the situation than I am. It's making both of our lives hard. We have to work together, and we have to find a way past this.

Me: How would you *like* your interactions to look or feel instead?

Elias: I'd like to feel like I have a partner, like we could collaborate on solutions rather than constantly butting heads. I'd like to know that our teams were working smoothly together rather than retreating to their corners because of the message we're sending.

Me: Well, that sounds pretty great. What do you think is getting in the way of that?

Elias: I can see that my heels are dug in. Hers are too. It might be keeping us both from seeing all the possibilities.

Me: What *is* another possibility for this relationship?
(*Long, long pause.*)

Elias: That we actually acknowledge that we are working towards the same goals.

Me: What's one thing you could do that would take you in that direction?

Elias: Well, meeting with her one-on-one might be a first step. I think we avoid it because we're avoiding each other, and that doesn't help. If I show her that I'm willing to listen and discuss her ideas, that could make her more open to a meeting.

Me: If you had that meeting, what could you do differently? (*Another long pause.*)

Elias: I could tell her how I would like our relationship to look and how our teams could work together differently—and how that would benefit the business, the people, and the two of us as leaders. If we can align on that, it might be a good starting point. It might help us get unstuck and become more open to each other's ideas.

Me: That does sound like a good starting point. Anything else you would do?

Elias: I can ask her if there is anything she'd like me to do differently and get feedback from her. Thinking about it makes me cringe, but I know it will help.

Me: Great. How do you feel about it?

Elias: A little nervous but hopeful. I'm actually excited to give it a try.

What did Wendy do to help Elias reach his own conclusions?

First, she helped him explore how he actually felt and what he really thought. The answer Elias gave initially about the problem with Brittany was surface-level and generic—it was "tense." Wendy could have assumed, based on that answer, that she knew what Elias meant or that *he* had already assessed the problem, but that would have been a mistake. **Asking somebody to "tell me more" gives them space to go a layer deeper,** to look at a challenge from a different perspective, and to be more transparent with what they think or feel. She also specifically asked him about his use of the word "tense." It's easy to fall back on vague language when we aren't sure how we feel or what we think. **Reframing or repeating what somebody says is a great technique** for helping them become more specific in their language *and* their thinking.

Once Elias was able to do that, Wendy asked, "How would you like it to look?" Throughout this book, we've asked you some version of the question, "What does success look like?" You can use it to **help the person you're coaching envision a better future state, consider where they want to go, and make choices about the endgame.** To expand their thinking, you can remind them that they don't have to know how to achieve their vision. You simply want them to feel motivated by it, because it will help them make more effective decisions as they move forward.

Wendy didn't share any possible solutions. She asked Elias what *he* thought he could do to achieve his envisioned future state. She used open-ended questions to help him come up with ideas that resonated with him and that he owned. (Again, we've provided a list of coaching questions at the end of the chapter.) As he presented ideas, **Wendy's only role was to encourage him to keep going.** Remember, if you narrow the person's options for responding by asking *limiting* questions that are based on your assumptions or opinions, you narrow their thinking.

Wendy also didn't ask Elias for a detailed plan. She asked him for one thing he could do, or a first step he could take. It's the same principle as our planning process—trying to focus on everything that would need to happen is overwhelming and disempowering. **Focusing on a few first steps to take is motivating and encouraging.**

At the very end, she asked him how he felt. This isn't a question most of us think to ask, but it's so important after somebody has done deep thinking. It helps them acknowledge the shift in emotion or perspective they've experienced.

When you're stuck, it can be hard to get unstuck on your own. But when you have the freedom to talk it out, especially with somebody who supports you in thinking the situation through and identifying a straight-forward next step to take, you suddenly feel free. You can play that role for anybody in your life. It just takes practice.

COACHING QUESTIONS TO HELP PEOPLE CLARIFY THEIR THINKING, GET UNSTUCK, AND TAKE ACTION

- Tell me more.
- I'm hearing you say X. Did I get that right? Anything else you want to say about that? *Reframing what you have heard gives them a chance to go deeper on that point.*
- What about this is important?
- How do you want this to turn out? *Or How would you like it to look?*
- What is the cost of this (conflict, situation, problem)? *You can help them along in their thinking by adding* "to the team" *or* "to the business" *or* "to the relationship."
- Is there another perspective you could choose?
- What is one possible solution? *Or What's one thing you could do that would make a difference?*
- What else could you do (or try)?
- What has worked for you in the past in situations like this?
- What do you already know you need to do?
- How do you feel now?

Imagine if you didn't have to feel like "chief problem solver" in your work or home life. Imagine one month from now, more of the people you care about are taking ownership of their challenges, coming up with solutions, and seeing you as the person who builds their confidence and then gets out of their way. Imagine how much of your time and emotional energy it would free up to devote to more important or more invigorating projects.

It takes unlearning old habits. It takes discipline, up-front time, and self-restraint. But the effort is *so* worth it. It will help you build better relationships, achieve bigger outcomes, and fuel your vision.

The Five Power Principles

Power Principle 1
DECLARE A BOLD VISION

Power Principle 2
CHOOSE A NEW PERSPECTIVE

Power Principle 3
PLAN THE WORK AND WORK THE PLAN

Power Principle 4
USE LANGUAGE OF ACTION

Power Principle 5
STOP TALKING AND GET CURIOUS

You've Had the Power All Along

Over the last 120-plus years, *The Wonderful Wizard of Oz* has been analyzed six ways from Sunday. Everybody has theories about its most important ideas and themes, and what it says about culture, politics, and more.

To us, it's about the power to create the life you want. At the end of the 1939 movie adaptation, Glinda shares her final bit of wisdom with Dorothy: **"You've always had the power."** That's the true message of this book and the true purpose of our work.

When the scarecrow asks Glinda why she didn't tell Dorothy that she had the power all along, Glinda said, "Because she wouldn't have believed me. She had to learn it for herself." Dorothy learned that she was capable and courageous, and she learned what was most important to her, what she wanted most.

Our intention has been to help you do the same. Chapter by chapter, we've explained the power you already have to create the life you want, this year and every year. We've given you a proven system for finding clarity, being bold, and taking action.

So now what?

We recognize that after more than two hundred pages, you may feel the same way some of our participants do: a little overwhelmed by the possibilities or unsure of how to begin. You're ready to use your power, but where do you start? By deciding what *you* want your life to look like one year from today. If you haven't already, **write your bold vision.** Your vision will be your north star, guiding how you spend your time and energy and motivating you to keep throwing your hat over the wall, even when it feels uncomfortable. It will guide you as you put the other four Power Principles into practice, so that you can do what you said you'd do and be who you said you'd be.

- If you've written your vision but you're feeling stuck or unsure of what to do next, ask yourself this question: "What's one thing I could do today?" Start there.

- Have you shared your vision or key parts of it with the important people in your life? If not, find at least one person to share it with, somebody who can support you and help hold you accountable.

- If you're telling yourself a disempowering story about a situation, a relationship, or even yourself, uncover the cost of that story and choose a new perspective.

- You might be thinking that there's never enough time to focus on your vision, or that you don't know what to do next. If so, take a close look at where you're being reactive rather than intentional and create your 90-Day Action Plan.

- If you can't seem to get other people onboard with your ideas or plans, raise your awareness of how you've been communicating. Start setting desired outcomes and preparing for your important conversations or meetings.

- Do you want to feel more connected with the important people in your life or spend less time mired in other people's challenges? Practice intentional listening techniques and help people solve their own problems—so that you're free to focus on your vision.

Taking all these steps over time is how to get on and stay on the path to the life you want, but what matters is that you start. We can almost guarantee that it won't always be comfortable, but over time, it will get easier—because the benefits of living a life of happiness, peace, and fulfillment make it worth it.

What's the alternative? A lot of waiting. Waiting for other people to step up. Waiting for circumstances to change. Waiting for more time. Waiting for your life to be different. You might be waiting for a long, long time. Instead, you could take responsibility for making it happen now.

Start somewhere, anywhere. Practice the habits we've described and use the tools we've shared. Over time, small changes will become big changes. To help you, we've created free resources on our website, https:// fastforwardgroup.net/book. We welcome any requests or recommendations for how we can support you better.

At the end of the day, it's up to you. You have one life, and it's your responsibility to feel lit up by it, to make it what you want it to be. You possess the power you need to create the life you want. What you'll find is that a world of possibility opens up when you start.

What are you waiting for?

Acknowledgments

In late 2012, when The Fast Forward Group was just a kernel of an idea, a very timely thing happened. Lisa got together with her former Viacom colleague, **Carolyn Everson**, who was heading up global sales at Facebook. Carolyn was concerned about how the pace, pressure, and burnout were affecting her people. She believed we could help and piloted Fast Forward. The impact exceeded her expectations, so she rolled out the program and executive coaching to thousands of executives at Facebook. Years later, she paid it forward by giving the program to their clients. We are eternally grateful to Carolyn—you are a true trailblazer.

Over the years, we have had the privilege to work with dynamic forward-thinking leaders who believe that when people are living their best lives, they do their best work.

David Lawenda, you are one of the most inspiring leaders we know. We appreciate your unwavering commitment to fuel your people and culture at Paramount.

To **Kristin Lemkau** at JPMorgan Chase, you are a force. After experiencing Fast Forward, you brought us in for countless conferences, programs, and Women's Leadership Day—impacting thousands of people at your firm. Creating the "Women on the Move" program with you and **Sam Saperstein** has been one of our most important and gratifying initiatives. Together, we have helped women to thrive and ascend.

To **Adam Baker,** a leader who cares so much about his people thriving at Amazon and in their personal lives. What a privilege to help you transform the culture and drive your movement.

To **Tara Walpert Levy,** who brought us into Google to work with your teams and women's networks for years and recommended us to others throughout the company. To **Blake Chandlee,** who brought us into TikTok—thank you for giving us the opportunity to work with some of the brightest young executives out there.

To **Jacki Kelley, Katherine Shappley, Martin Ott, Greg Glenday, Marta Martinez, Tim Castelli, Jeff Howard, Michelle Klein, Patrick Harris, Andy Marcell, Amy Armstrong, Jessica Bishop, Pam Kaufman, Mita Mallick, Arun Bedi, Julie Eddleman, Katie Fogarty,** and **Sarah Iooss,** thank you for supporting us and being our raving fans!

To our Fast Forward graduates who we interviewed for this book—there would be no book without your stories. Thank you for being vulnerable. Your challenges and triumphs will inspire readers to use the 5 Power Principles.

To all the Fast Forward graduates who threw your hats over the wall and created the life you want—keep going!

To our Fast Forward team: what a special work family we have created. Thank you for sailing the ship while we were writing this book. Thank you for caring so deeply about our work, our clients, and each other. You inspire us every day.

To **Debbie George,** our first employee and the heart of our company. Thank you for your countless hours writing and editing to make the book an engaging read that captures the magic of Fast Forward.

To **Marina Lvova,** thank you for all the feedback and encouragement while on your maternity leave! To **Courtney Tripp,** you've been essential from early reads to our public launch, and you never missed a beat, even while campaigning for public office.

Lari Bishop, there would be no book without you. Thank you for your patience, wisdom, skill, and perseverance. Thank you for putting up with two inexperienced authors with strong points of view! We are incredibly lucky to have worked with you.

And last, but definitely not least, a huge thank-you to our families, and in particular, to our husbands, **Gary Leshgold** and **Sean McCarthy**. You have supported us in building a business from scratch while also raising children, managing your careers, and dealing with millions of other things. For the many hours you spent listening to us, supporting us, guiding us, and handling all the stuff when we weren't there, even when your own plates were overflowing, we are eternally grateful. We know we hit the jackpot with you guys.

Notes

Chapter 1

1   Joris Lammers et al., "To Have Control Over or to Be Free From Others? The Desire for Power Reflects a Need for Autonomy," *Personality and Social Psychology Bulletin*, March 16, 2016, available at https://journals.sagepub.com/doi/abs/10.1177/0146167216634064?rss=1.

2   Emily Ekins, "What American Think About Poverty, Wealth, and Work: Findings from the Cato Institute 2019 Welfare, Work, and Wealth National Survey" report published by Cato Institute, 2019, available at https://www.cato.org/publications/survey-reports/what-americans-think-about-poverty-wealth-work#downloads.

3   David Robson, "How to Restore Your Sense of Control When You Feel Powerless," BBC.com, December 14, 2020, available at www.bbc.com/worklife/article/20201209-how-to-restore-your-sense-of-control-when-you-feel-powerless.

Chapter 2

1   Frank O'Connor, *An Only Child* (originally published in 1961; quoted edition: New York: Open Road Media, 2014, combined with *My Father's Son*), 150.

2   Peter Senge, *The Fifth Discipline*, revised edition (New York: Currency, 2006), 143.

3   D. Kahneman and A. Tversky, "Prospect Theory: An Analysis of Decision Under Risk," *Econometrica* 47, no. 2 (March 1979): 263–291, https://doi.org/10.2307/1914185.

4   William Samuelson and Richard Zeckhauser, "Status Quo Bias in Decision Making," *Journal of Risk and Uncertainty* 1, no. 1 (March 1988): 7–59, https://www.jstor.org/stable/41760530.

5   Janina Larissa Bühler, Rebekka Weidmann, Jana Nikitin, and Alexander Grob, "A Closer Look at Life Goals Across Adulthood: Applying a Developmental Perspective to Content, Dynamics, and Outcomes of Goal Importance and Goal Attainability," *European Journal of Personality* 33, no. 3 (2019): https://doi.org/10.1002/per.2194.

6   Martin Seligman, *Learned Optimism* (New York: Vintage, 1990), 76–77.
7   Rick Hanson, *Buddha's Brain: The Practical Neuroscience of Happiness, Love, and Wisdom* (Oakland, CA: New Harbinger Publications, 2009), 41.
8   Elizabeth Kensinger, "Negative Emotion Enhances Memory Accuracy: Behavioral and Neuroimaging Evidence," *Current Directions in Psychological Science* 16, no. 4 (2007): https://doi.org/10.1111/j.1467-8721.2007.00506.x.

Chapter 3

1   Rosamund Stone Zander and Benjamin Zander, *The Art of Possibility: Transforming Professional and Personal Life* (New York: Penguin Books, 2002), 26–27.
2   Stephen R. Covey, *The 7 Habits of Highly Effective People*, 30th Anniversary Edition (New York: Simon & Schuster, 2020), 109.
3   Jeffery Pfeffer, *Dying for a Paycheck* (New York: Harper Business, 2018), 8.
4   Ingrid Fetell Lee, "Ever say 'I'll be happy when . . . ?' Here's why you need to stop doing that—now," Ideas.TED.com, June 15, 2022, available at https://ideas.ted.com/why-you-should-stop-saying-ill-be-happy-when/.

Chapter 4

1   Dominican University press release, "Study Focuses on Strategies for Achieving Goals, Resolutions," available at https://scholar.dominican.edu/cgi/viewcontent.cgi?article=1265&context=news-releases, and Gail Matthews' research summary, available at https://www.dominican.edu/sites/default/files/2020-02/gailmatthews-harvard-goals-researchsummary.pdf.
2   E. Tory Higgins, "Shared Reality: What Makes Us Strong and Tears Us Apart," Oxford Scholarship Online, Oxford University Press, November, 2019.
3   Katy Milkman, *How to Change* (New York: Portfolio, 2021), 177.
4   Vanessa Buote, "Most Employees Feel Authentic at Work, but It Can Take Awhile," *Harvard Business Review*, May 11, 2016; Ralph van den Bosch and Toon W. Taris, "Authenticity at Work: Development and Validation of an Individual Measure at Work," *Journal of Happiness Studies* 15, no. 1 (January 2013): doi:10.1007/s10902-013-9413-3.

Chapter 5

1   Jon Acuff, *Soundtracks: The Surprising Solution to Overthinking* (Grand Rapids, MI: Baker Books, 2021), 26.
2   Marcus Aurelius, *Meditations: A New Translation*, transl. by Gregory Hays (New York: The Modern Library, 2002).
3   Peter Wason, "On the Failure to Eliminate Hypotheses in a Conceptual Task," *Quarterly Journal of Experimental Psychology* 12, no. 3 (1960): 129–140, https://doi.org/10.1080/17470216008416717.
4   C. R. Mynatt, M. E. Doherty, and R. D. Tweney, "Confirmation Bias in a Simulated Research Environment: An Experimental Study of Scientific Inference,"

Quarterly Journal of Experimental Psychology 29, no. 1 (1977): 85–95, https://doi.org/10.1080/00335557743000053.

5 Ulric Neisser and Nicole Harsch, "Phantom Flashbulbs: False Recollections of Hearing the News About Challenger," chapter in *Affect and Accuracy in Recall,* Emory Symposia in Cognition (Cambridge, UK: Cambridge University Press, 2010).

6 Leslie Hausmann, John Levine, and E. Tory Higgins, "Communication and Group Perception: Extending the 'Saying Is Believing' Effect," *Group Processes & Intergroup Relations* 11, no. 4 (2008): https://doi.org/10.1177/1368430208095405.

7 Carol Dweck, *Mindset: The New Psychology of Success* (New York: Random House, 2006), 59.

Chapter 7

1 Stephen Klemich and Mara Klemich, *Above the Line* (New York: Harper Business, 2020), 39–40.

2 Susan Sorenson, "How Employees' Strengths Make Your Company Stronger," Gallup, available at https://www.gallup.com/workplace/231605/employees-strengths-company-stronger.aspx.

3 E. A. Vogel, J. P. Rose, L. R. Roberts, and K. Eckles, "Social Comparison, Social Media, and Self-Esteem," *Psychology of Popular Media Culture* 3, no. 4 (2014): 206–222, https://psycnet.apa.org/doi/10.1037/ppm0000047.

4 Karen Baikie and Kay Wilhelm, "Emotional and Physical Health Benefits of Expressive Writing," *Advances in Psychiatric Treatment* 11, no. 5 (September 2005): 338–346, https://doi.org/10.1192/apt.11.5.338.

5 Heidi Koschwanez et al., "Expressive Writing and Wound Healing in Older Adults: A Randomized Controlled Trial," *Psychosomatic Medicine* 75, no. 6 (2013): 581–590, doi: 10.1097/PSY.0b013e31829b7b2e.

6 Naomi I. Eisenberger and Matthew D. Lieberman, "Why It Hurts to Be Left Out: The Neurocognitive Overlap Between Physical and Social Pain," in K. D. Williams, J. P. Forgas, & W. von Hippel, eds., *The Social Outcast: Ostracism, Social Exclusion, Rejection, and Bullying* (New York: Psychology Press, 2005), 109–127. Also, see David Rock's SCARF model of social threat and reward.

Chapter 8

1 Jim Kwik, "The Hidden Cause of Burnout," Inc.com Real Talk Videos, available at https://www.inc.com/video/jim-kwik-the-hidden-cause-of-burnout.html.

2 Greg McKeown, *Essentialism: The Disciplined Pursuit of Less* (New York: Crown, 2014), 25.

3 Laura Vanderkam, "There's a Better Way to Reclaim Your Time Than 'Quiet Quitting,'" *New York Times* (Opinion), September 13, 2022, available at https://www.nytimes.com/2022/09/13/opinion/burnout-quiet-quitting.html.

Chapter 9

1   David Allen, *Getting Things Done: The Art of Stress-Free Productivity* (New York: Penguin Books, 2002).
2   Phillippa Lally et al., "How Are Habits Formed: Modelling Habit Formation in the Real World," *European Journal of Social Psychology* 40, no. 6 (October 2010): 998–1009, https://doi.org/10.1002/ejsp.674.

Chapter 10

1   William Ury, *The Power of a Positive No* (New York: Bantam, 2007), 7.
2   Ury, *The Power of a Positive No*, 27.

Chapter 11

1   Siemens Enterprise Communications and SIS International Research, "SMB Communications Pain Study White Paper," https://www.sisinternational.com/smb-communications-pain-study-white-paper-uncovering-the-hidden-cost-of-communications-barriers-and-latency/.
2   Kerry Patterson, Joseph Grenny, Ron McMillan, and Al Switzler, *Crucial Conversations* (New York: McGraw-Hill, 2012), 4–6.
3   Marshall Goldsmith, "Reducing Negativity in the Workplace," Ask the Coach column, *Harvard Business Review*, October 8, 2007, available at https://hbr.org/2007/10/reducing-negativity-in-the-wor.
4   Guy Winch, "Does Complaining Damage Our Mental Health?" *Psychology Today*, January 19, 2012, available at https://www.psychologytoday.com/us/blog/the-squeaky-wheel/201201/does-complaining-damage-our-mental-health.

Chapter 12

1   Leslie Perlow, Constance Noonan Hadley, and Eunice Eun, "Stop the Meeting Madness," *Harvard Business Review*, July–August 2017, available at hbr.org/2017/07/stop-the-meeting-madness.

Chapter 14

1   Kate Murphy, *You're Not Listening* (New York: Celadon, 2019), 19.
2   Katharina Kircanski, Matthew Lieberman, and Michelle Craske, "Feelings into Words: Contributions of Language to Exposure Therapy," *Psychological Science* 23, no. 10 (October 2012): https://www.ncbi.nlm.nih.gov/pmc/articles/PMC4721564/.
3   Heidi Godman, "Can Friends Who Listen Help Protect Your Memory and Thinking Skills?" *Harvard Health*, November 1, 2021, available at https://www.health.harvard.edu/mind-and-mood/can-friends-who-listen-help-protect-your-memory-and-thinking-skills.
4   Nancy Kline, *Time to Think* (Cassell Orion, 1999), 15.
5   Andrea Zaccaro et al., "How Breath-Control Can Change Your Life: A Systematic Review on Psycho-Physiological Correlates of Slow Breathing," *Frontiers in Human*

Neuroscience 12, no. 353 (September 2018): https://www.ncbi.nlm.nih.gov/pmc/articles/PMC6137615/.

6 Jing Jiang et al., "Neural Synchronization in Face-to-Face Communication," *Journal of Neuroscience* 32, no. 45 (November 2012): https://doi.org/10.1523/JNEUROSCI.2926-12.2012.

7 Francesca Gino, "The Business Case for Curiosity," *Harvard Business Review,* September–October 2018, available at https://hbr.org/2018/09/the-business-case-for-curiosity.

Chapter 15

1 Katy Milkman, *How to Change* (New York: Portfolio, 2021), 252.

2 Adam Grant, *Think Again* (New York: Viking, 2021), 157.

Resources

At https://fastforwardgroup.net/book, we share a robust workbook that will help you get the most out of this book, including

- Exercises to put the Power Principles into action
- Sample visions
- Additional tools and resources

Index

About the Authors

Photo by Angelique Hanesworth

Lisa McCarthy was at a career crossroads after twenty-five years leading sales organizations at Viacom and Univision that were responsible for billions in revenue. After a significant reorg at Univision, Lisa chose to take a big risk. Rather than pursue another sales leadership position, she "threw her hat over the wall" to create a company that would help people achieve their ambitions and dreams—regardless of the circumstances. She saw the high cost of the always-on pace and pressure as well as the common tendency to deprioritize well-being and happiness and put important things on hold. She knew it could be different, and she set out to create a program to help make that change possible.

Her first call was to her friend **Wendy Leshgold**, who she met at age ten in sleepaway camp. Wendy was at her own crossroads. After a decade in advertising leading teams at Ogilvy & Mather, BBDO, and Deutsch and another

Photo by Art Streiber

decade as a Co-Active Training Institute–certified coach with her own executive coaching practice, she was looking for a way to make a more out-sized impact. When Wendy told people she was no longer taking clients, they thought she was nuts to give it up, but Wendy knew this would create the opening she needed to find the next thing. And when that call came from Lisa, she knew this was it.

Together, they launched The Fast Forward Group, with a mission to transform workplaces and lives. They are known for their energizing, research-backed programs and executive coaching that take a whole-life approach to growth, success, and happiness, helping people achieve their full potential in the face of any circumstances. They've worked with tens of thousands of executives from successful companies around the world, including Amazon, Google, Facebook, Disney, TikTok, Paramount, Visa, Ford, JPMorgan Chase, Colgate, Aon, and more. Their approach has been featured in *Forbes* and in high-profile podcasts. They regularly speak in front of large audiences for companies and associations.

Wendy is a highly active board member of California Environmental Voters. She lives in Los Angeles with her husband and three children. She can often be found hiking the hills and walking with her beloved dogs. You can connect with her at

LinkedIn: in/WendyLeshgold
Instagram: @WendyLeshgold

Lisa lives an "overly fulfilled" life in Port Washington, NY, with her husband and three children. She can often be found hiking or on a tennis or paddle court. You can connect with her at

LinkedIn: in/LisaMcCarthyFFG
Instagram: @LisaMcCarthyFFG

And you can connect with Fast Forward Group at:

FastForwardGroup.net
LinkedIn: @the-fast-forward-group-llc
Instagram: @fastforwardgrouptraining
Facebook: @thefastforwardgroup